"...nds-on guide for helping any business differentiate ...aking customer service to a new level at every level. ...ling lessons presented in an interesting easy to read and ...y to implement format."

— **Roger J. Dow**, Former Marriott Executive and President & CEO of Travel Industry Association of America (TIA)

"*License to Serve* should be retitled *License to Succeed.* Simple, clear, engaging, informative. Easy to use, understand and implement. *License to Serve* moves to the top of the required reading list for everyone in Irving responsible for creating the impressions and delivering the services that allow us to live the brand promise we make to every visitor."

— **Maura Gast**, Executive Director Irving TX Convention & Visitors Bureau

"In our increasingly competitive profession, providing optimum service to our clients is the difference between success and failure. For that reason, *License to Serve* is required reading for all new associates and staff."

— **Robert G. Hicks**, Managing Partner Javerbaum Wurgaft Hicks & Zarin

"Common sense skills written in common language that anyone can apply."

— **Joseph Perri**, Vice President, Investments Montauk Financial Group

"Good customer service is no miracle. This book and its strategies will help you and your team of employees make your customers feel like champions."

— **Jim Craig**, 1980 Olympic Gold Medalist U.S. Hockey "Dream Team" Goalie Motivational Speaker

"The loss of one customer translates into the loss of thousands in revenue for my company and that is unacceptable. Read *License to Serve*, implement their strategies and you'll be on your way to earning and keeping customers for life."

— **Mark T. Elia**, President, Mark of Excellence Remodeling, Inc.

"With *License to Serve* Doug and Joe have followed up their first book — *License to Sell* with another example of how to strive for excellence in your organization. At ARAMARK Harrison Lodging, we use *License to Sell* as the foundation for our Sales Training. We will take full advantage of *License to Serve* to make sure that we excel in maintaining the Environment of Optimum Customer Service."

— **Mike Fahner**, Vice President of Marketing & Development
ARAMARK Harrison Lodging

"Doug and Joe craft a compelling case that the basic truths of good customer service are self-evident."

— **Peter Shure**, Director of Strategic Marketing
Conferon Global Services, Inc.

"A sequel to the best-selling *License to Sell*, this new book effectively demystifies the lost art of customer service. Practical and entertaining, *License to Serve* provides relevant and insightful examples and exercises designed to improve core competencies. I highly recommend this easy-to-use book for training and staff meetings of any organization. As the service sector continues to grow, those without this book will be ill-prepared for the most significant economic development force of the 21st century."

— **Dr. Richard Harrill**, Senior Business Associate
George Tech Economic Development Institute

"Doug and Joe have delivered an exceptional and practical resource for busy professionals who really care about customer service. You will find yourself marking up pages and referring back often."

— **Mike Gamble**, President/CEO
SearchWide "Executive Recruitment Experts"

"Great service is not a dying art. On the contrary, It's alive, well and even more vital to organizational health than ever before. What is dying is the traditional approach to developing effective service strategies…and the insights found in this book will help you discover why."

— **Peter Yesawich**, Chairman & CEO
Yesawich, Pepperdine, Brown & Russell

"*License to Serve* defines in a straightforward yet entertaining way what all outstanding business enterprises know. . . that great customer service is a guaranteed path to success."

— **Michael D. Gehrisch**, President & CEO
International Association of Convention & Visitor Bureaus

"There is no such thing as customer insurance, but this book is the closest thing to it."

— **Carmel King**, Vice President & Group Publisher
IMAS Publishing, Inc.

"After the sale comes the service. *License to Serve* is all you need to delight your customers. Read it, Apply it, PROFIT!"

— **Nancy & Kevin Boyle**, Owners
Budget Blinds

"The art of customer service is masterfully outlined in *License to Serve*. Utilizing the steps brought to life in this book will ReGenerate your organization's/company's focus on the customer."

— **Mike Sadeghpour**, President, ReGenerate
"Positive Results Through Positive Psychology"

By Joseph C. Ilvento & Doug Price

BOOKS

License to Sell

By Joseph C. Ilvento

BOOKS

Nobody to Somebody in 63 Days or Less

MONOGRAPH

Selling Strategies for Changing Economic Times

JOE ILVENTO / DOUG PRICE

LICENSE TO SERVE

BEYOND SELLING...
THE HOW-TO GUIDE
FOR CREATING
EXCEPTIONAL
CUSTOMER SERVICE

Applied Business Communications, Inc.
New Jersey

Acknowledgment

We would like to thank Tracy Ilvento, who invested her editorial, design and publishing skills in this book. Without her interest and support, this book would still be in bits and pieces on our brains and hard drives.

ABC, Inc. 29 Maple, Suite 100, West Long Branch, New Jersey 07764

tracyilvento@comcast.net

ISBN 0-9654362-3-3

*To our wives who experience customer
service daily and inspired us
to write this book. It is through their
experiences, insights, and suggestions
— coupled with our own — that provide
the rich context for this book.*

JOE ILVENTO

Joe Ilvento has been serving customers – both internal and external – since working in his family's restaurant at age 10. Keeping customers happy and beyond satisfied is the secret to his success. It is as much an art as it is a science. The art is seen in Joe's attitude of service. Ask anyone he has ever known or worked with, he is always looking to help and go beyond what is expected. Working in the family restaurant business he saw first hand the impact of word of mouth advertising and repeat customers. His grandfather and father also knew how to treat customers. Long after they retired from the business, barely a day goes by when Joe introduces himself and the person says, *I used to eat at Ilvento's restaurant,* followed by stories about how his father and grandfather did things to make them feel special. Twenty years after the restaurant's closing, Joe still hears these stories – now that's customer service! You could say he learned these lessons in the trenches from some of the best.

Sales and service go hand in hand. Joe, upon graduation from Syracuse University with a Bachelor of Science degree in psychology, began his career with Cable & Wireless Communications. Within a few short years he was promoted to National Sales Trainer. He then moved on to become a Master Trainer with Learning International (formally Xerox Learning Systems) – one of only 13 worldwide. In 1989 he started his own consulting firm and has been helping Fortune 500 clients ever since. In 1998 one of them, the largest financial firm in the world, hired him as an executive in their corporate offices and he continues to play a major role in helping others in the areas of executive development, talent management and staffing. Delivering service excellence inside the corporation is something Joe does on a daily basis.

Joe has personally presented to over 15,000 business people around the world and has presented via self-directed online learning modules to another 20,000. Past audience members have included numerous government agencies such as the Central Intelligence Agency, the Marines, the Air Force, the Treasury Department, the Secret Service, and Army National Guard. Private sector audience members have included Citibank, MCI/WorldCom, Printing Industries of America, the National Real Estate Institute of America, Marriott, First Union Bank, Royal Insurance, Bechtel, the Family Research Council, Ford Motors, and more.

Joe's first book *Nobody to Somebody in 63 Days or Less* shows people how to use word of mouth advertising and referral selling to dramatically increase sales. Joe partnered with Doug Price on his second book *License to Sell — Professional Field Guide to Selling Skills & Market Trends*. He has appeared in newspapers, magazines and on various radio and television shows including the *Bloomberg Financial Network*, *WPGC Business News Radio*, *Entrepreneur's Radio Showcase*, and the *Business as Unusual* television show.

Joe Ilvento specializes in developing the selling, marketing and customer service skills of others. His seminars are interactive, applied, fun, and most of all effective. Joe can be reached at 1-800-382-6343 or by e-mail at joeilvento@comcast.net.

DOUG PRICE, CMP

Doug Price is an authority on sales, marketing, and customer service. For more than 25 years, he has sold everything from Fuller Brushes and executive coaching to meetings and conventions. Doug's approach to sales and service was shaped with direct sales jobs as a teenager and in large-part by 18 years of selling conventions for Marriott International. His passion for sales earned him numerous sales incentive awards and Doug was named Marriott's Rookie Director of Marketing of the Year in 1983. He also served as Marriott's Vice President of Employment Marketing and Director of Sales Training and Development. In 1995, he founded his own business, Keystone Consulting, with a focus on sales training, management development and customer service improvement. In 1998, he merged his company with The Miles/LeHane Group, a prominent career management firm, where he served as president.

Doug feels that his philosophy towards sales and service was shaped very early in life. His father, Harry Price, was a salesman his whole life, primarily selling ranges and kitchen appliances for Caloric and Tappan. As a child, Doug was introduced to many of his dad's clients throughout his sales territory in Ohio. Doug enjoyed riding in the car with his dad on sales calls. His dad mixed business and pleasure very well. Often the Price family entertained customers in their home and vice versa. Those early lessons on building relationships stayed with him.

Like many successful salespeople, Doug started early in sales with a newspaper route delivering a "free weekly paper." As a carrier, the only way to make money was to try and collect the "suggested donation" of 50 cents per month. The only reason people would pay for a free weekly paper was if the carrier placed the paper exactly where the customer wanted it each Wednesday morning. The carrier also had to be persistent in following up to catch people when they might be home to pay. Doug learned customer service and timely follow-up delivering "free papers" and consistently winning sales contests among carriers.

Selling Fuller Brushes at the age of 15 taught Doug how to handle rejection and use testimonials. As he would work door-to-door getting rejected, he realized that sales are a numbers game. Not everybody was going to buy and you couldn't take a "NO" answer personally. Instead, he learned to be happy that he didn't waste time giving a sales pitch to an uninterested buyer. Once Doug made a sale, he would tell the next person he called on what their neighbor up the street had purchased. When the neighbor heard what someone else had decided to buy, selling became easier. Testimonials are still very powerful today in selling.

Selling Marriott Hotels, Resorts, and Suites for eighteen years crystallized the importance of building and maintaining relationships with customers. In the highly competitive world of hotel sales, properties compete to convince meeting planners, along with business and leisure travelers to stay at their facility. Anyone who travels knows there are hotels everywhere and the choices range from no frills to full frills. Doug found that getting to know his customers as well as their needs was a key element in separating him from his competition. Customers buy the salespeople as well as their products/services — and the better you know a customer - the more likely you willmake a sale. Doug has actually had the honor of delivering a eulogy at a customer's funeral. That represented a true relationship!

Today, Doug Price is Senior Vice President of Professional Development for The International Association of Convention & Visitor Bureaus in Washington, DC. He is responsible for life-long learning, professional certification, accreditation, and academic affairs. He is a recognized public speaker and speaks around the world to audiences on a variety of sales and customer service topics. Doug is also the co-author of *License to Sell*, a book on "high-touch" selling in a "high tech" environment which now serves as the text for IACVB's online sales course @ www.gwutourism.org/destinationselling.htm.

If you need sales or customer service presentations that are customized and interactive, contact Doug Price at 202.296.7888 or by e-mail at dprice@iacvb.org.

CONTENTS

Section Two

WHO IS RESPONSIBLE FOR CUSTOMER SERVICE

Section Three

DETERMINING CUSTOMER SERVICE TOUCH POINTS

Section Four

MAINTAINING AN ENVIRONMENT OF OPTIMUM CUSTOMER SERVICE

APPENDIX

Foreword

by

Duane Knapp — President, BrandStrategy, Inc.

From my perspective, exceptional service should be the rule, not an option. Our brand research worldwide clearly indicates that if an organization has a real promise and every employee believes it is their job to deliver the brand's promise, you'll most likely enjoy doing business with them as a customer!

License to Serve is a practical, easy to use guide for implementing a wide variety of successful customer service initiatives. This book is all about a "license" to make customers feel great... "to give every employee permission to delight customers and go beyond what's expected. Every customer wants to feel special and when

License

1. Deviation from normal rules, practices, or methods in order to achieve a certain end or effect.

2. Latitude of action, especially in behavior or speech

3. To give off permission for somebody to do something; for an activity to take place.

4. Official permission to a person or group to own or do something.

5. The opportunity to do something especially when this goes beyond normal limits.

6. The freedom to rearrange the facts of ordinary life to make a more striking effect.

they do, the employee feels wonderful because it appeals to their higher motives."

At the end of the day, it's all about how your customer's feel not necessarily the process or the protocol. The *License to Serve* is dedicated to the concept that service is about providing pleasant surprises, extraordinary responses and going the extra mile.

Exceptional customer service is all about the higher motives i.e. feeling of fulfillment, helping others, essential goodness. So figure how you want your customer to feel and then only hire employees that really enjoy making other people happy!

We believe that regardless of an organization's so called service commitment, it's essential that everyone commits to the same promise! The promise defines how an organization wants its customers to feel. It is not necessarily the same as an advertising slogan.

In Starbuck's case, the promise of "the third place"; i.e. first place home; second place office and the third place, where you go to indulge yourself, relax, getaway, hang out, etc. is the key to their success.

Any size organization can use the *License to Serve* to improve customer service. Exceptional service is not a program or this years "strategy du jour", it's all about a mindset and a lifelong commitment to the experience!

Here's your challenge; give a copy of *License to Serve* to every employee who works with you and begin the journey to ultimate success!

Duane Knapp is President of BrandStrategy, Inc, which advises leading brands worldwide. He is considered the source for creating Genuine Brands and the author of the award winning book, *The BrandMindset®*, available in many languages.

Great Truths of
Optimum Customer Service

This section presents 65 customer service truths to help you deliver *optimum customer service* – going beyond customer satisfaction. These insights, observations, techniques, tips, strategies, and tools are the first step in crossing the line between your customer satisfaction expectations and *optimum customer service* from the customer's perspective. If you believe...

The customer shouldn't have to seek out service, it should come to him.

Customers seem to get it right every time. They know the difference between good service and bad, caring employees and non-caring employees, and when they are dissatisfied

Customer service success is determined by the customer — not the employee or company.

Attention to small details can make all the difference; small details generate big results.

In the customer's eye...customer service perception is customer service reality.

One of the secrets to delivering service is learning how to listen and learn from customers. Only by putting aside your need to be heard can you really begin to listen and learn.

Always error on the side of service.

...you're on the path towards customer service success!

Customer Labels

What do the following labels have in common?

Patient

Client

Guest

Passenger

Patron

Shopper

Ticket Holder

Fan

Member

Partner

Tourist

Attendee

Voter

Citizen

Customer

These are labels given to people by the world we live in. You can be labeled many of these in the same day as you deliver and receive service. Although the label may change many times, expectations of how customers want to be treated or served do NOT change. Herein lies a dynamic business principle that successful organizations and business owners abide by:

Give customers what they want

when they want it;

It's sometimes all right to give more –

but never give less than what customers expect!

If your business makes it their mission to always meet or exceed expectations in every single customer encounter, you will separate and differentiate your business from all of your competitors. ■

YOUR MISSION

Review the list of labels at an employee meeting, but intentionally skip those that apply to your business. Ask employees what their service expectations are when they are wearing each particular label. Then, choose the labels that do apply to your specific business and ask what the service expectations are of your customers. Capture the list and then have employees rate how they do on meeting customer's expectations. In each case, have a discussion around what barriers exist that prevent expectations from being met and develop a plan to eliminate those customer service barriers.

#2

———

Customer Value — Girard's Law of 250

One of the best Customer Service laws ever written was by Joe Girard who said, if you get a customer mad at you, you can bet he is going to bad mouth you to 250 people over the course of time. Think about it, if you make an enemy or handle a customer poorly, anytime you, your business name or your product or service comes up in a conversation, you can be sure this irate customer will tell his story.

Bottom line — keep your customers happy. Make sure you do your best to resolve with complete satisfaction each customer service issue that surfaces. Understand that for each one you don't, 250 people will hear about it!

If you are a small business owner or operate within a small market niche — 250 customers lost can put you out of business. ■

#3

Lifetime Value of a Customer

Understanding the lifetime value of a customer is something every customer service rep should know. We sometimes only think of the customer as a one time transaction. Depending on the products or services you support that could be the case. However, most products or services have a "life" associated with them where at sometime in the future, the product or service will have to be replaced or renewed, upgraded or serviced in some way.

Let's assume a customer complains to a local restaurant that the take out meal he ordered the day before did not match the order he placed. Let's say there was mayonnaise on the sandwiches when there should have been mustard. Let's also say the cost of the order was $5. A person handling this complaint may say what's the big deal, mayo vs. mustard and refuse to give the customer credit for such a minor error. In the customer service representative's eye the business loses a $5 customer right? Wrong.

Let's assume that customer gets upset because the business refuses to refund the order. He also decides that he will no longer do business with you and use the deli across town. Let's also assume he orders a sandwich once a week. The lifetime value of that customer is $5 x 48 weeks (at work) x 10 years = $2,400. The $2,400 is the lifetime value of that customer.

Lose just ten customers in a year, you now have to make up $24,000 in lost sales. Make sure you consider the lifetime implications. Is it worth saving $5 on principle and losing $2,400 in potential lifetime value? If you stand strong on your principles, you may not be in business at all! ■

#4
—

Knowing How Much to Invest in a Customer

In any customer relationship it is always a difficult decision to determine how much you invest either to gain and/or maintain the customer relationship. One technique to help you answer this question is to measure the return of the customer to you. Return can be determined over a lifetime or based on a single transaction. Past history of your product or service and how it is purchased will determine which end of the spectrum you measure.

Obviously, you would not want to invest more in the customer than the customer's lifetime return to you, unless, there were extenuating circumstances (e.g., a loss leader). An exception to allowing the maintenance or acquisition cost to exceed the value of the customer is when the customer can be leveraged to gain or keep new or additional customers. The fact that you do business with company ABC and the fact that ABC is a well respected firm may be a reason why new and existing customers do business with you. ■

#5
—

Knowing the Cost of Service Problems

As a customer relations professional you should be acutely aware of the cost associated with recovering from specific service problems. Knowledge of this cost will provide you and your staff with an incentive, not to incur them but also to understand the impact on the company or the customer in the event a problem occurs.

In the hospitality industry, an example of this is the 30% food cost plus labor on the cost of a meal. Another way to look at this is to understand your "margin" or "profit margin." In the food industry, it ranges from 10% to 25%. In other words, for every dollar the customer spends, if you operate at a 20% profit margin, you earn 20 cents. Conversely, for every dollar you lose, refund or comp to the customer – your cost is 80 cents. ■

#6
——

Every Service Has a Price

It is important that you and your customer service staff understand that every service you offer has a price associated with it. This knowledge will insure the solution for a customer service problem doesn't exceed the profit associated with it. Often times, a customer solution might involve a series of small services that when looked at individually do not appear to be great. However, it is only when you identify and track these expenses do they begin to add up.

The customer must understand and in some cases be reminded about the value and cost associated with the services you provide. If no value is perceived on behalf of the customer, it makes the customer service solution that much harder and the customer feels entitled to a solution that may involve discounts, rebates or money back. ■

#7

Your Value of Service

Think of your service as a premium. If someone were to pay you for the customer service you deliver, what would it be worth? Often customer service is viewed as part of the sale – included in the cost of goods sold. A game you can play with yourself to keep motivated, focused and delivering the best customer service you can – customer after customer – is to put a dollar number on each interaction.

Pay yourself for efficiency in getting the customer the answer he called for.

Pay yourself for how well you connected with the caller on a personal level.

Pay yourself a percentage of any money the customer will save as a result of the information you provided.

Pay yourself all the money the company saves as a result of the service you provide.

Although just pretend money, at the end of each day you will be hundreds – maybe even thousands of dollars richer. ■

#8
—

Measuring the Profitability of Customers

One strategy for continued customer growth is to apply "Preteo's Law" of 80/20. This means that 80 percent of your business will be generated by the top 20 percent of your satisfied client base. Analyzing the profit and expenses associated with each of your existing customers allows you to rank your customers in terms of profitability.

In some cases, it may cost you more to keep the customer than to drop them. This may result from a variety of reasons:

✓ A customer who was at one time a large one has now become a small customer.

✓ The customer you thought would evolve into a large customer continues to place small orders.

✓ A customer may require a lot of personal attention and services outside of your normal procedures and therefore incur a lot of hidden or ancillary costs.

Some companies even go as far as carefully examining the bottom 20 percent of their existing customer base to determine whether or not they should remain as customers. Not to say that you would instantly drop your bottom 20 percent, but earmark them for individual review. Specifically, the review would include past history, future potential and a general marketing strategy as how to go about increasing their annual revenue with your firm. After all if you apply Preteo's Law some of those bottom 20% may be generating 80% of your costs. ■

#9

Perception of Trust, Comfort and Credibility

Comfort levels and overall trust of you, the company and the transaction process will enter into the customer service process due to the proliferation of electronic sales and service methods. Decisions will still be made based on facts – price, services, features, benefits, warranties, and guarantees – but more than ever, the decision will be based upon the perceptions of trust, comfort and credibility of you and your company.

Before optimum customer service can occur, the customer is already questioning what could happen:

✓ Who can I trust?

✓ Have I done business with this salesperson or company in the past?

✓ Did they do a good job?

✓ Can I trust them again?

✓ What if they don't perform as expected?

✓ What is my recourse? ■

YOUR MISSION

How to you currently instill trust and credibility? Consider policies, procedures, the physical environment.

Contact five customers and request a testimonial on customer service and support? How and where can you use the testimonials?

#10
___

Create a Virtual Presence

The world wide web has created a new business environment that breaks down traditional size barriers. In the virtual world, competing businesses or stores become equal in size – limited only by the size of the customer's computer screen. Smaller businesses have the opportunity to create the perception of trust and credibility and compete against larger competitors.

Just because you are the biggest and best in the physical world, doesn't mean it will translate into the virtual world. B. Dalton and Barnes & Noble continue to spend millions on physical retail locations. However, if I ask you to name a virtual bookstore, you would probably say Amazon.com. What are you doing to become the virtual leader in your industry? ■

YOUR MISSION

How can you transfer that trust and credibility to a virtual environment?

Does your web site look as trustworthy and credible as your biggest competitor? Why not? What can you do to bring yours up to speed? What can you do to bypass your competitors?

#11

——

Creating a Doctor-Patient Relationship with Customers

W hen customers call with problems they should experience the same trust and confidentially as they have with their doctor. However, trust is something that must be earned with the customer. For trust to occur, the customer service person must listen carefully, ask intelligent and probing questions designed to uncover the symptoms and potential source of the problem, and then diagnose and prescribe a mutually acceptable solution. Just like a doctor-patient relationship it is important that you allow the patient to participate in the process. If you feel that the doctor doesn't have a genuine understanding of the problem it is causing you, any advice or recommended treatment the doctor provides will be in doubt.

Good customer service departments keep a history of their customers similar to good doctors. Good customer service departments often schedule regular check-ups to insure customer health and satisfaction. Treat your customers like patients and they will live forever. ■

#12
___

Always Ask – May I Help You?

How pushy is too-pushy from a customer's perspective? On one hand customers don't want a pushy salesperson or service rep hovering over them, but on the other hand they want help if they need it. You should always error on the side of service. Always ask, "May I help you?" If the customer says no, simply reply, "I am here if you need me, please do not hesitate to ask." If you happen to see what the customer is interested in, you might say, "There are similar products like that one over here" or "That item is on sale – 20% off."

What you are doing here is leaving the door open for the customer to make the next step. Often, the customer will find it difficult to resist learning about specials especially if they are related to the product at hand. Even if there is no special, create one on the spot. It doesn't have to be dollars off. It could just be a new product that was stocked, or a new model, or sale on similar items, or the fact that if they open a charge account they get 10 percent off the item in hand.

When a customer walks through the front door, someone – if not all personnel – should make eye contact and be conscious of whether or not someone has asked the person if they need help. A general rule of thumb for any service person is never walk by a customer unless you ask to help, make eye contact, etc. Create a contest in-house with a mystery shopper and give $10 to the employee who asks "do you need help" first or notices non-verbal buying signals that a customer may need help or has a question.

Think how satisfied you would feel if every time you had a question there was someone in sight who could help answer your question. Remember, the customer shouldn't have to seek out service, it should come to him.

One way to accomplish this is by having greeters stationed at the door to ensure everyone who enters the store gets this personal service and eye contact. Wal-Mart is famous for this and does it all the time, not just during the holidays or as a gimmick. ■

#13

Lines Are Hidden Opportunities

One Saturday morning, my then 10-year-old daughter Sarah and I were standing in line at our local bank. Due to ATM's and e-banking, many of you probably have not stood in a bank line for quite some time! The line was not moving at all and the customer dealing with the teller was obviously frustrated over the transaction. After what seemed like five to six minutes, Sarah looked around the bank and noticed a man wearing a suit and tie sitting in a back office reading a newspaper. She asked me, "Dad, do you think that is the manager back there reading the newspaper?" I said yes, probably. She then asked, "What business does he think he is in?" What an insightful question! I thought about it and said, "He thinks he is in the bank business, but he sure isn't showing it is he?" Sarah shot me a look and said, "He should be in the – managing the line business at his bank." Yes, I am her proud father but I feel Sarah nailed a key issue. The bank manager could have been out front assuring the customers in line that everything would be moving along shortly. Or, at least finding out how he could help his teller. What if the manager got behind the counter and handled the next customer? What a concept!

Do you have a business that requires your customers to wait in lines? One of the most frustrating things to customers is a long line. Deli counters have a system in place that is easy to incorporate. By taking a number, the customer is allowed to take a seat, shop or do something else but stand idle in line.

This approach would work at consumer product return counters and anywhere people gather in line only to wait for service.

Loews Hotels manages the three resort properties at Universal Studios in Orlando. They are Portofino Bay, Hard Rock and Royal Pacific. Loews did its homework and discovered people do not like to wait in lines for anything these days. With that in mind, there are two important benefits their resort guests enjoy that make it worth staying with them. First, between shuttle boats and buses, there are virtually no lines to stand in for more than 15 minutes to get back and forth between the park and resorts. Second, and most important, each guest receives his or her own personal Key Card. Most of the attractions and shows at Universal Studio have two entrances to get in – one for the masses and one marked Express. All you have to do as a guest of one of the Loews Resorts is to show the Key Card at the Express entrance of each attraction and you avoid waiting in line for the normal 45 to 60 minutes! For a family of four, we figured out that we saved 12 hours a day NOT standing in lines. That gave us more time to enjoy the park!

Smart restaurants have introduced the beeper system to mange the wait and allow you to shop or sit uncomfortably nearby until a table is ready. Amusement parks have signs that set the wait expectation from this point. They also make waits visually stimulating to build the excitement about the upcoming ride. The message on hold is a similar concept. ■

YOUR MISSION

How can you under promise and over deliver on a waiting line?

What activities do your people do that may send the wrong message? (Letting the phone ring, socializing, eating)

Customers who need service want action. One of the easiest ways to get customers moving towards a solution is to get them doing something.

#14

Explain How Things Work

When interacting with a frustrated customer who has a problem, many times their frustration is due to your lack of understanding of their problem.

One of the best ways to offset this frustration is to keep the customer informed. When on the phone, simply explain what you are doing. For example, "If you'll just bear with me for a few seconds, I will pull up your file in our computer. I am entering your name now, the computer is searching, ah there you are Mr. Jones. I see you ordered an xP 42, is that correct? This narrative approach to customer service is preferred compared to dead silence. The customer is left to hang on the phone or watch you stare at a screen not knowing if you are surfing the net or actually helping solve the problem.

Use a narrative approach when a process is complex or will take time to solve such as finding a late product. Always explain any benefits associated with the solution, such as procedures to double check, any quality review, an inspection point, or tracking numbers. ■

YOUR MISSION

This is a perfect time to role play a frustrating customer interaction. Assign both the customer and employee roles to staff members. Rather than make up a problem, have the customer role use an real issue or one they have experienced.

Ask them to recreate the problem for you. Or, ask them to tell you their story. How does the employee respond?

Make sure the employee's series of steps or actions are relevant to the situation and are methodical in nature. The flow should be logical and obvious to the customer. If it is not obvious, prior to asking the customer to take action, tell the customer why you want them to do what you want them to do. Document the process. The thoroughness of questions should be dependent on who picks up the phone.

#15

Invite People Back

A fter resolving a problem, thank the customer for his purchase. Express confidence and enthusiasm that the customer will return to make additional purchases. "I look forward to seeing you here again, we appreciate your business and if there is anything I can do to help with your next visit, please don't hesitate to ask for me. My name is Joe."

People like to feel appreciated and wanted. You would be surprised how many people do come back as the result of an invitation and even more exciting is how many people will ask for you by name. For example, while picking up lunch at Wendy's drive thru window, the employee replied "See You Tomorrow."I did! ∎

YOUR MISSION

What are you saying to invite customers back?

#16
___

Greet Your Customers Like Guests in Your Home

If you work in an environment where you interact with your customers in a face-to-face format, you should always greet your customers as if they were guests in your home. Smile, answer the door (call to service) promptly, keep eye contact, and act as if you are glad to be with them. In some cases it may even be appropriate to offer them a drink or a seat or some other service available to you.

You may start the conversation with a little small talk or ask, "What can I do for you?" The point here is that you want to immediately create an atmosphere of service – an atmosphere where you are there to serve the customer. Guests are welcome and should not be viewed as an interruption in your day. If a customer walks in he should take precedent over any side conversations you may be having with other employees. One of the worst examples of customer service and one that definitely broadcasts the wrong message is when a customer approaches two employees. The employees are talking and continue talking with the customer standing idly by. I have been in situations where the conversation went on for minutes. You could imagine the decisions that are made by the customer during that time about whether or not he will do business with the company again in the future. Bottom line customers take precedent over employee conversations.

Greet the customer, make him or her feel at home, introduce yourself, and extend an offer to help. Think of each customer you work with as a favorite rich aunt or uncle who you only get to see every few years. I say "rich" because, after all, don't your customers pay you? Isn't a portion of your check in some way their money? However, in this case your payback is the service you are able to provide to the customer. ■

#17

———

Break the Ice to Form a Bond

Customers want fast and friendly service. However, service that is too fast can sometimes make the customer feel rushed and make the event impersonal. One of your goals as a customer service representative should be to build relationships. Not personal relationships – although those are ok – but a relationship with the company or product. Many customer service interactions are one-time events. The customer and service rep meet once by phone or in person, never to see each other again. To begin the interaction you may wish to spend a moment on small talk.

The amount of small talk should be in proportion to the time you will spend with the customer. The quicker the service the quicker the small talk. A simple and genuine "Good morning," or "How are you?" may be enough to break the ice. Another way might be to ask the question "Were you waiting long?" The weather, sports, a compliment about an article of clothing or jewelry are all ways to break the ice. Remember to introduce yourself when on the telephone. If in person, wear a name tag. You have one minute to make a connection with a customer, why not have all the variables in your favor?

By creating some kind of relationship – no matter how small – it shows the customer that you are human. More than this, it creates a bond so that the customer is more likely to accept your outcome even if it is not positive. ∎

#18
___

Using People's Names

When embarking on a customer service call, do your best to introduce yourself and get the name of the person to whom you are speaking. Use your best judgment as to whether or not to use Mr. or Ms. Although it is usually best to do so if the person is more senior than you in either age, position, or the item discussed has significant value associated with it. It may be awkward to have a 20-year-old customer service rep say Mr. or Ms. to a customer his own age or younger. It's not normal and may appear to be insincere.

Use the customer's name when you first begin a conversation and again periodically throughout the interaction. Finally, always end the conversation using the person's name. It shows respect and shows that you are attentive to the matter at hand.

Business cards are effective tools when using people's names. When presented with a person's business card, don't immediately put it in your pocket. Take a moment to read it completely. You might find points of interest to discuss such as the town, their title, the spelling of their name, or area code.

Also while speaking to the person keep the card cupped in your hand so you can glance at it if you forget their name. This is much less obvious than removing the card from your pocket. ■

#19

The Power of Listening to Customers

W e have all been communicating throughout our life as a child, student, employee, manager, and if applicable a spouse or parent. A breakdown of the communication process reveals the time we spend in an average week on each aspect:

Writing	10%
Reading	15%
Talking	30%

LISTENING 45%

What is interesting is that we only listen effectively approximately 25% of the time. For now, let's define effective listening this way:

✔ taking in information while remaining non-judgmental and empathetic;

✔ acknowledging the talker in a way that invites the communication to continue; and

✔ providing limited, but encouraging input to the talker's response, carrying the person's idea one step forward.

We actually hear close to 70,000 words a day of noise! A novel is normally 50,000 words. That means we are hearing almost a book and a half a day of words! What we all need to learn is when and how to listen more effectively. We all have room to improve our listening habits. The bottom line is the more I listen . . . the more I learn.

Listening is a powerful force in all human relationships. When an employee listens effectively to a customer, it is a way of saying, "you are important and I'm not judging you." In turn, customers who are being listened to appreciate the employee doing the listening. Why? Acknowledgment is a basic need. Customers are more likely to respond positively to a person who meets this need than to someone who does not.

Test Your Listening Knowledge. Next to each statement, note whether you think the statement is true or false.

___ When a listener's emotional level is high, he or she will be an effective listener.

___ Speaking is a more important part of the communication process than listening

___ Because listening requires little energy, it is easy

___ Listening is an automatic, involuntary response

___ Hearing and listening are the same skill

___ The speaker is completely responsible for the success of communication

___ People listen every day. This daily practice eliminates the need for listening training

___ Competence in listening develops naturally

___ When people learn to read, they simultaneously learn to listen

___ Listening is only a matter of understanding the words of a speaker

If you said false to each statement, you are a good listener.■

#20

Levels of Listening

All of us listen at different levels of effectiveness throughout the day. The effectiveness at which we listen depends greatly upon factors such as:

✓ Conflict in a situation

✓ Dealing with emotions

✓ Criticism being directed at them

✓ When they are being disciplined

✓ When feeling anxious, fearful, or angry

Listening can be divided into three levels, characterized by behaviors:

Level 1— 100% Attention: I will not judge the talker but will place myself in their position and attempt to see things from their point of view.

Examples include acknowledging and responding; not allowing distractions; paying attention to someone's total communication; being empathetic to the speaker's feelings and thoughts; great eye contact; active body language i.e., leans into a conversation and shows focused energy.

Level 2 — 60% Attention/40% Other: I am hearing the talker's words, but also thinking about other things such as what I will say next.

This person listens logically, being more concerned with content than feeling emotionally detached which can lead to a dangerous misunderstanding because the listener is concentrating only slightly on what is being said. Therefore, speakers may be lulled into a false sense of being listened to and understood: "deer in the headlights" look.

Level 3 100% Non-Attention – I am listening. I am daydreaming.

This person follows the discussion only enough to get a chance to talk: quiet and passive without responding; false attention while thinking about related matters; making judgments; forming rebuttals or advice; preparing what they want to say next; more interested in talking than listening; preoccupied; selfish; no eye contact. ■

MISSION

In the space below list three or four behaviors you would observe from a person who is listening at each level.

Level 1 _____

_____

_____

_____

Level 2 _____

_____

_____

_____

Level 3 _____

_____

_____

_____

Most people will agree that level 1 is the ideal level. Why are so many people at level 2 and 3 most of the time? Some reasons may include:

✓ They have never been trained

✓ Are unaware of their listening habits

✓ Never have made a serious effort to improve their own listening skills

✓ It is easier to talk than it is to listen

✓ It takes time and energy to listen

✓ Effective listening has not been modeled to them

Keep in mind most people listen at all three levels throughout the day. The more time you spend listening at level one, the more effective listener you will be. Be aware of your listening levels at all times. Remember, only by putting aside your need to be heard can you really begin to listen and learn.

What kinds of professional jobs require their people to be outstanding listeners to be successful? How about some of these:

911 operators

Air traffic controllers

Counselors

Teachers

Doctors

Judges

Juries

Lawyers

Waiters

Taxi cab drivers

Think about the consequences when someone in one of these professions fails to listen effectively. The point is that it is difficult to come up with a profession where listening does not play a key role in being successful. ■

#21

Overcoming Effective Listener Obstacles

What blocks us from listening? Often it is our own ego. With an enormous need to be heard, our egos overwhelm any desire to hear. As a person charged with delivering outstanding customer service, do you ever think you know the answer to a customer's need – just because you have faced this same situation in the past? Keep in mind that situations, just like customer's needs, do change. Put your ego aside and listen carefully to someone's needs.

Obstacles include:

✓ Your ego

✓ Talk too much

✓ Interrupt others

✓ One upmanship

✓ Word speed and paraphrasing

✓ Environment (too loud, too quiet, bad connection)

✓ Physical state (sick, headache, medication, age)

Listening to others gives us information. INFORMATION IS POWER! Effective listeners are able to concentrate and find the most valid information in whatever they hear. So, how do you overcome this ego block? Develop a burning desire to listen and learn in every situation you face daily. Remember the basic principle: Only by putting aside your need to be heard can you really begin to listen and learn. Abraham Lincoln once said it is better to remain quiet and be thought a fool than to open your mouth and remove all doubt. ∎

#22
—
Talk Too Much?

Why do we talk so much? We have all been invited to talk since birth. The need to talk *at* people versus *to* people can normally be attributed to nerves. How would you know if you were talking too much? Do you ever catch yourself saying these expressions?

✓ Are you listening to me?

✓ Did you hear what I said?

✓ Now, listen to what I'm going to tell you!

✓ Listen up now; pay attention.

Do you ask yourself:

✓ What is so interesting behind me?

✓ Why am I losing eye contact with this person?

✓ Do I keep interrupting every time the other person starts to talk?

✓ Am I not taking a breath or pausing every couple of sentences?

If so, practice giving the gift of silence. The goal for your talk time in any conversation with a customer should be on average 50%. Otherwise, you are not learning as much as you could from the customer about his or her needs and wants.

A person providing customer service is in some ways similar to a salesperson making a sale. In order for either to provide what a customer needs or wants, be certain you understand what a customer needs. You do this by asking questions and getting the customer to open up and talk. To avoid talking too much and dominating a conversation, have questions prepared that get the customer talking. Here are sample questions that you might apply:

- ✓ How can I help you?
- ✓ What size or color?
- ✓ Have you been here before?
- ✓ What is your current modem speed?
- ✓ Do you have the name of the person you spoke with earlier?
- ✓ Would you like my assistance now?
- ✓ Shall I get that for you?
- ✓ How has it worked for you?
- ✓ What would you like us to do for you?
- ✓ Who is involved in the process?

Generally speaking, use who, what, where, why and when type questions to get an open ended customer response. Use do, does, did, are type questions to get a limited, concise or more closed end response.

It is very important to practice effective listening as the customer answers these questions. These types of questions, along with others specific to your industry, will get the customer to speak and help prevent you from talking too much. Give the gift of silence! ■

MISSION

Make a list of sample questions that are related to your industry:

1_____

_____

2_____

_____

3_____

_____

4_____

_____

5_____

_____

6_____

_____

7_____

_____

8_____

_____

9_____

_____

10_____

_____

#23

━━━

Do You Interrupt Others?

D o you find yourself interrupting others or are you tempted to interrupt others with your thoughts? Do you finish statements and sentences of slower, more deliberate customers to try and save time? Interrupting and finishing customer's sentences is a turnoff. If you think you know what someone is going to say – let them say it! Give the gift of patience! Patience is an important ingredient for open communication. You may hear statements and sentences that start off with . . .

✓ Where can I find . . .

✓ What we really need is . . .

✓ How soon can you ship . . .

✓ When will you deliver . . .

✓ The last one we had . . .

✓ I am not sure about . . .

✓ I need to talk with . . .

Until the customer finishes his or her thought, be patient. Listen for audible punctuation such as periods and question marks. Until you hear that final pause, button your lip. You might want to count to three after someone has finished a thought. It not only ensures the customer has stopped talking, but it allows you to gather your thoughts. If interrupting is a big issue for you, and if this is appropriate, keep a glass of water or coffee close by and "sip as they speak." It is nearly impossible for you to talk and drink at the same time! Give the person time to deliver a complete message.

Take your understanding a step further by clarifying and confirming the customer's message. You might say, "Just so I am crystal clear, what you need is..." or "Tell me more." ∎

#24

One Upmanship

This listening block allows your ego to drive your response. Oftentimes your comment can come across as being superior to someone else's. What is dangerous about one upmanship is it can turn a customer off quickly. As an example, suppose a customer in a golf store states that his best drive was 280. Don't one up and say, "I drive it 300 yards on a bad day." Say, "Wow, that's great. Isn't it a good feeling when you know you're hitting your best. I know how you feel." Align with the customer – share a common experience or emotion. Don't one up it and destroy the bond.

The way to overcome one upmanship is to give the gift of interest. This is easier said than done. Show a genuine interest in the customer by asking questions that get them talking about their goals such as:

✓ What type of driver do you use now?

✓ Do you know anyone who plays with this new driver?

✓ Where did you hear about it?

✓ How do you think this driver could help your game?

✓ Are you left or right handed?

✓ How much golf do you play?

Do you see that the employee is showing a genuine interest in the customer? It is not about how well the employee uses the driver. It is all about how the customer would like to use the driver. Put the ego aside and give the gift of interest. ∎

#25

Thought Speed & Paraphrasing

If your mind is racing ahead of a customer, you will not be able to effectively respond to someone's total communication. You will miss communication signals from a customer. It is very easy for your mind to race ahead because of something called "thought speed." On average, a person can speak nearly 200 words per minute. As a listener, you can process words at the rate of 300 to 500 words per minute. This is why, when people tell you to think before you speak, it makes sense because you do have the ability to do it! How you manage "thought speed" will keep you engaged in conversations with customers and help prevent your mind from wandering off and daydreaming.

If appropriate, one proven way to manage thought speed is to take written notes to be used as memory joggers. Realizing that everyone is not in a position to take written notes, try clarifying the meaning of what someone is saying as they are saying it. When the person is finished with their complete thought, attempt to paraphrase what the person has just said. In the golf example, it might sound like this; "So what I heard you say is that you would like a driver with a bigger club face, is that right?" The customer will either say yes or no. If he or she says yes, that proves to them that you are listening and understand what they are looking for. If the customer says no, go back and probe further. The additional interest you show will pay great dividends in the world of customer service. ■

YOUR MISSION

Test your listening skills! After reading the following twelve questions, give yourself a score from 5 (always) to 1 (never). Consider each question in a work environment as opposed to how you listen with family and friends. When you finish, add up all the individual numbers to come up with your total score. Then check your total score against the inventory scale.

1. Do you find yourself understanding the meaning of what was said?

   Always 5   4   3   2   1 Never

2. Do you stop what you are doing and give your full attention when listening?

   Always 5   4   3   2   1 Never

3. Do you concentrate on what a customer is saying and blockout external distractions such as noise and movement?

   Always 5   4   3   2   1 Never

4. Do you effectively read customer's body language?

   Always 5   4   3   2   1 Never

5. Do you give customers appropriate eye contact, head nods, and other non-verbal cues to illustrate you are listening?

   Always 5   4   3   2   1 Never

6. Do you withhold judgment about a customer's idea until he or she has finished speaking?

   Always 5   4   3   2   1 Never

7. Do you respond to a customer non-judgmentally if you do not agree with him or her?

   Always 5   4   3   2   1 Never

8. When a customer hesitates, do you try to encourage him rather than begin your reply?

   Always 5   4   3   2   1 Never

9. Do you listen fully even if you think you know what the customer is going to say?

   Always 5   4   3   2   1 Never

10. Do you allow a customer to finish before preparing your response?

    Always 5   4   3   2   1 Never

11. Do you question the customer to to clarify his or her idea more fully when you do not have a complete understanding of his or her thought?

    Always 5   4   3   2   1 Never

12. Do you restate/paraphrase what the customer said and ask if you got it right?

    Always 5   4   3   2   1 Never

Add up the numbers from all 12 answers and write your total score: _____

LISTENING INVENTORY SCALE

Total Score

55 – 60 Expert listener: Congratulations! You do your best to listen effectively and take the time and effort to make sure you have a complete understanding of the customer's message.

45 – 54 Good listener: You tend to listen when you think the content of the message is important. However, in certain situations or with some customers, you may not use all your listening skills. Pick a question or two where your score was three or less and develop an action plan to use the skills on a daily basis. Continue improving your score until you score in the 55 – 60 range.

35 – 44 Need improvement: Identify your lowest ratings and determine what factors influenced your response. Does it affect your job and those around you in your work environment? How would you personally benefit if you can dramatically improve your score? Pick two or three questions where your score was three or less and develop an action plan to use the skills on a daily basis. Continue improving your scores until you score in the 50 – 60 range.

34 or less Poor listener: Assuming you took the inventory seriously, you need to immediately improve your ability to listen. Pick two to three questions where your score was less than three and develop an action plan to use the skills on a daily basis. Continue improving your score until you score in the 45 – 60 range.

YOUR MISSION

How does listening feel?

Think about the following statements:

How do you feel when someone really listens to you?

How do you feel when someone shows interest in you through eye contact and clarifying and confirming questions?

_____

_____

You would think of words such as important, cared for, confident, good, respected.

Now think about this statement:

How does it feel when you invest 100% attention into listening to someone else?

_____

_____

You would likely think of words such as challenging, focused, tiring.

The point is that it feels good to be listened to and it takes some effort to listen to others. It is easier to talk than it is to listen.

#26

Ethics and Customer Service

Maintaining a strong ethical relationship with your customers is important. Deceptive advertising, bait and switch techniques, releasing customer addresses and phone numbers, and any form of communication to the customer that is not genuine will almost always lead to lost customers. With the advent of computers and the Internet, customer privacy is more important than ever before.

If you have not done so already, define some ethical guidelines around your product or service. Items may include: sharing of personal information about your customers with other parties; return policies; advertising and marketing promotions; collection policies; telemarketing guidelines; sale dates; refund policies; credit policies; rates of interest; opt in and out of e-newsletters.

Publish this "Privacy Notice" for your employees to read and understand. Make it part of your culture and include it in your training sessions. Place the "Privacy Notice" in a public place where your customers can see it such as waiting areas or showrooms or access it on your web site.

A recognized firm in Internet Marketing, usdm.net, offers the following best practices regarding email contact:

✔ Do not send an email that is longer than the e-mail window.

✔ Address the person in a friendly, but professional manner.

✔ Use bullet points to make the email more of a quick read.

✔ Include salient points in the email message itself and not in an attachment.

✔ Use an appropriate subject line and always modify the subject line when you reply to show that the same subject is followed, but now with some new information.

✔ Always use an email signature with your phone number and full contact information.

✔ Always use spellcheck! ■

#27
▬▬▬

When to Fire a Customer

Ideally, you never have to get to this point in a customer relationship. However, there are times when a customer's demands go too far or other factors require you to fire a customer. When a customer is fired, more often than not there is no going back nor a possibility that this customer will return to do business with you under current conditions. It is a tough decision and one that should have measurable and objective criteria surrounding it.

Naturally, one must take into consideration any laws associated with who you can and cannot do business. Assuming that you abide by all local, state and federal laws, you may have additional criteria to define what constitutes firing a customer. Questions you might ask include:

✓ Has the customer fallen below minimum order or dollar amounts?

✓ Is there any minimum dollar amount?

✓ Are there any shipping constraints, in state, out of state, out of country?

✓ Does the customer's demands exceed profit for the transaction

✓ Is there a poor payment history and failure to pay invoices?

✓ Is there a balance due on past accounts?

✓ Does the customer abuse or monopolize the customer service or sales representative's time?

✓ Is the customer dishonest?

✓ Does the customer harass your employees?

When firing a customer it can be done on the spot, in a face to face, telephone transaction, or mail. If the reason for wanting to fire the customer is a result of an internal audit or change of strategy, can be done in the form of a letter. In general terms, you should outline the reason for cancellation of the customer's account, and if desired you may identify what changes the customer must make to remain a customer in good standing. When putting something like this in writing for any reason, have an attorney review the letter because it could come back to haunt you if it becomes a legal issue.

Language and tone should be neutral, specific and non-negotiable. Customers will respect the fact that you have both a process and minimum standards by which you do business.■

#28

▬

Mirror the Customer

When trying to identify with the customer and address any customer service related issues, try mirroring the customer. This mirroring techniques works both on the phone and in person.

To mirror:

Speak at the same rate of speech as the customer – if the customer is a fast talker, pick up your pace. If the customer is a slow talker – slow down your pace.

Re-use key words and terms the customer uses to describe the problem. If the customer says he has a concern with your product, don't re-label it a problem. Call it a concern too. You might say, "Well Mr. Jones, let's see what I can do to remove that concern with our product. I'll need to start by asking you a few questions, is that OK with you?"

Adjust the volume of your speech to mirror that of the customer. If the customer is a loud talker, raise your voice a little. If a soft talker, reduce your volume.

Mirror the body language of the person erring on the conservative side. If the customer is leaning forward at the table you may want to do the same. If the customer tends to put his hand on his chin when he thinks, you may wish to do the same.

The key behind mirroring is not to mimic the other person but to let them see a little of themselves in you. Most people like people like themselves. These techniques – if used subtly and in the right environment – can be a very powerful way to make an instant bond with your customer.

Service should always be done with a smile. Just as you can mirror the customer. The customer can mirror your manner both in person and over the phone. You can change a person's attitude just by smiling back at them. ■

#29

Ask for Referrals

It is amazing how many customer service representatives (CSR) do not solicit referrals. The CSR has a valuable opportunity to help create more business by asking for referrals. Make it easy by instituting a customer referral program. Either mail it to your customers or allow your reps to explain it to the customer when appropriate. Don't ask for a 100 names, just one or two and make it easy for the customer to respond.

To help prime the pump, you might end the interaction by saying something like:

"This month we are running a referral program. If you provide the name and phone number of one person we can call and use your name we will give you XXX. If you provide us with the name of three people we can call and use your name we will give you XXX, YYY and ZZZ. All I need is a name and a phone number and the gift is yours."

These prequalified leads would be provided to the sales team. If only 20% of 100 people responded with a name that is like cold calling 200 or 300 people. The closing ratio of the sales team will be much higher on these referred prospects because they are not cold calls, but warm calls made to a friend who may need the product or service. ■

#30

━━━

Put On a Happy Face: Smile

This sounds simple to do, but look at your customer service colleagues. Do they begin each customer service interaction with a smile? Even if you are on the phone, a smile should always be the first step in every customer service call. When visiting large customer service facilities and call centers, we often see mirrors next to the phone aimed at the phone rep. Why? Not to make sure their hair is in place, but to help remind the rep to begin each call with a smile. Smiling goes hand-in-hand with a positive, upbeat tone. You need to project confidence in your company, product, and of course the service you can deliver.

There are only a few times when the smiling happy, positive approach may not work. Such situations might include a very irate customer, someone who is very emotional, or someone you genuinely believe would act negatively if you come off as too positive. In these cases, a neutral tone and simply friendly facial expressions should be substituted.

Hire the smile! If you have people meeting and greeting customers, make sure their natural disposition is a "happy looking" one. Some people are born with a smile on their face. You want those people who are always laughing, smiling and enjoying life to greet your customers. ▪

#31

Handling Irate Customers

Your ability to handle irate customers is a skill. You have to be part psychologist, part machine, part mother, and part customer service rep. In other words, you may have to use a variety of skills to sooth the customers' emotions and bring them back to "happy customer" status.

When customers are irate, do your best to remain calm. Understand that they are not irate at you personally (at least they shouldn't be), but at the company or the product that has caused them grief. Speak gently and deliberately. If it is an option, you may wish to bring the customer to an area where other customers will not overhear the exchange.

The first things you must do are align and empathize with the customer. From there you must move the conversation into a resolution phase so the customer feels that something tangible will be done to resolve the issue. If it is an option, you may even gently ask the customer, what would they like to see done to resolve the situation. Remember no promises here – it is just a way to get a benchmark of what it will take to get the customer back to neutral. Should the customer offer a suggestion – and it is one you can act upon – reconfirm it in your own words, "So if we do _____ you would be satisfied?" Should the customer confirm, you should be quick to resolve the situation. If you get a no, continue to clarify and confirm until you have a customer suggested solution on the table that is mutually acceptable to you and the customer.

If the customer asks for too much in return, suggest some alternatives that could work. If possible build off of or modify slightly the ideas the customer offered so as to keep the customers fingerprints on the solution. The more customer fingerprints, the more likely the customer will accept.

If you are still at an impasse, calculate the "lifetime value" of the customer (see previous chapter). If the lifetime value of the customer far exceeds the value of the customer's demand, you should concede to the customer's demand. If you are unsure whether or not the customer will do business with you in the future, you may have to get a future purchase commitment on paper and make it legal and binding. ∎

#32

Rapid Response

One surefire way to get a customer more upset about a problem is to offer a slow response time. Often times when a customer has a problem with your product or service, there is a cost to him as a result of that problem. To help minimize the cost and impact your product or service has on the customer, you should rapidly respond to any and all customer concerns. A rapid response can take many shapes including:

✓ A phone call to the customer to acknowledge the problem

✓ A timeframe as to when the problem will be fixed

✓ If you have customer or employee suggestion boxes, check them every day and acknowledge all suggestions within 24 hours

✓ Make a second effort call to ensure satisfaction

✓ Make spot calls after purchases (and deliveries) especially to customers who have experienced problems in the past. This can help head-off problems before they escalate

When faced with a customer complaint, you can use this opportunity to solidify your relationship with the customer. It is during these critical moments in a company-customer relationship that determine the basis for future business. When you handle the customer complaint correctly and effectively – and if possible exceed expectations – you will have a customer for life. ■

#33

Own the Problem

O ne of the first things customers want when they contact a customer service rep is for that person to take responsibility and own the problem. They want to feel that their issue is being addressed and is being given the attention it deserves. Proactive, leadership-based statements such as, "Let me take that on as an action item and get back to you with more information" or "Since we caused the problem, we should own it. What if we did..."   or "I will personally see this problem through the tracing process and get back to you with my findings."

When you get out in front and take ownership of the problem early in the customer service process, you will see a noticeable shift in the customer's attitude. After all, how can you argue with someone who is now an advocate of yours and who is going to personally be working on your behalf?

Just one word of caution. If you agree to own the problem – own it. Punctual follow-up and seeing the problem through to resolution can some time takes hours, days or even weeks to resolve. However, seeing it through to a positive end is a very rewarding customer service experience. The customer will forever be in debt to the rep and a personal bond especially between the customer and rep often emerges. Just try to make the number of times where you have to go to these lengths far and few between with the same customer.

If you do have to hand the problem to someone else, explain the problem first and note the customer's name, situation and any relevant information needed to resolve it. This will ensure the customer feels you care and will prevent him from having to explain the problem all over again.

When you deliver optimum customer service, customers will leave happier when a problem is resolved beyond their expectation than if they experienced no problem at all! ■

#34

Practice Handling Problems

When not on the phone or handling customers on a face to face basis, customer service reps should spend time practicing their skills on one another. One way to do this is to think about the 10 most common objections and problems you receive on a regular basis. Then, role-play them with a partner.

Sharing various approaches and techniques on how to handle a particular customer or problem situation will provide your customer service team with multiple approaches designed to lead toward customer service success. Often times, the customer may reject the first or second solution you offer to fix the problem and having three or four or more different ways to approach the same issue can mean the difference in keeping the customer and losing one. ■

YOUR MISSION

What are some common problems raised by customers?

_____

_____

Use these as the basis for this "Fish Bowl Exercise" at a staff meeting. Pick one person to play the role of customer and another to begin the customer service interaction. Allow the first person to begin and then after a minute or so have the customer pick someone else to continue the dialog. Continue circulating until everyone has had a chance to offer their solution. This is a great exercise to share different styles and create a sense of team camaraderie.

#35

Easy Access

The ability for your customer to access your customer service is critical. Making access to service is becoming easier and easier. Telephone automated response systems and the Internet allow for 24 hour a day 7 day a week customer service options. Couple this with email or voice mail and you have a very powerful, interactive 24/7 support system. Although your business may not be open 24 hours a day or seven days a week, at worst a customer reply is 12 to 48 hours away. Many companies will designate one rep to monitor email and voice mail systems on a periodic basis during "off" times to bring that response time down to as little as an hour. Systems can even be programmed to ring a paging device. Thus, the "on call" person could respond immediately to any critical issue that arises.

How quickly you respond to a customer will depend on the products and services you provide. An order for new office supplies probably can be able to wait until Monday morning, but a broken water pipe in the middle of winter will require immediate attention.

Are you easy to reach? Do you offer your customers a toll free number to reach you? With more metropolitan areas slicing and dicing their cities in different area codes, it can be frustrating for a customer to figure out what number to call. An 800 or 888 toll free number is one way to maintain consistency with your phone number. Advertise this number in the phone book along with your local number, business cards, stationery, and other visual locations such as the Internet under your regular number. If your number spells something, always include the digits next to the letters to make dialing easy. Vanity numbers, as they are often called, are great for radio advertising or when you are just trying to commit a number to memory. However, these numbers can be an obstacle when they are offered as the only option. You make the customer enter into a matching game that requires them to start all over if the number they enter doesn't correspond to a matching letter. The customer then has to hang up and redial two or three times from a home phone or worse yet from a cell phone while driving. To say the least, the customer will not be in a "buying" mood when he gets through and if he has a problem with your product or service, you just made it worse.

It's easier than ever to stay in touch with customers when they need you most because of call forwarding, cell phones, 800 or toll free numbers, voice mail systems, pagers, wireless email, the Internet and other electronic devices. ■

#36
___
Email

E mail is a great tool to use with customer service. It allows the customer to say exactly what he or she wants and can articulate the exact nature of the problem. The customer also has the ability to attach a picture or other document that may help illustrate the problem or question at hand.

An email address is a must if your customers have access to computers when using your product or service. On the receiving end, configure your email in-box in such a way as to signal you when new mail arrives. Treat email just as you would a customer standing in your place of business or a telephone call. When responding have attachments ready that may be useful to the customer. Such attachments might include: answers to frequently asked questions, step by step instructions, graphical illustrations and even coupons or discounts towards future purchases.

Keep drafts of pre-written emails with attachments in your draft folder. This allow you to quickly provide information that the customer needs via email. It is very powerful when you can say, "If you check your inbox, it should already be there." ■

___

YOUR MISSION

Do you give customers the option to opt in or out of future emails?

_____

_____

_____

Do you ask customers if they prefer a phone call or email to respond to their issue?

_____

_____

_____

Do you send follow-up email to ensure the customer is indeed satisfied?

_____

_____

_____

#37

Voice Mail

Voice mail has changed the business landscape almost as dramatically as email. It allows both parties to communicate with each other when one party is unable to answer the telephone call personally. Those who use voice mail to deliver optimum customer service use it to provide information on your status, location and availability. Updated voice mail messages can be an asset if used correctly to deliver a message and obtain information for timely follow-up. The problem occurs when people use their voice mail to hide from customers.

There is a danger here that you can cause more distrust if you don't follow-up ASAP. On the voice mail message be clear as to when people can expect a response and do it. George Zimmer of the Men's Warehouse has built an entire advertising campaign around the voice mail messages he gets regarding the great service delivered in his stores. Can your company make the same type of claims?

If you tend to get a lot of voice mails, give the customer an option to prioritize their message. After all, if it is very important, you'll want to hear and address the issue sooner than later.

If you're in a situation where you can leave a voice mail message for a customer, this is a good way to communicate your service at the customer's convenience. ■

YOUR MISSION

Do you and your employees know how to update their voice mail messages?

_____

_____

_____

Do you have a policy on return calls? If not, create one.

_____

_____

_____

Ask customers if they received a timely response to their call?

_____

_____

_____

#38

Follow-Up Means Follow-Up

One of the biggest pet peeves many customers have about customer service is the lack of follow-up. When a promise is made it should be kept. If you are going to say you are going to call back by noon – call back by noon – even if you do not have anything to report. Good follow-up is timely and should be done in a logical and professional manner.

Follow-up can occur in the form of a phone call, letter, email, or face-to-face encounter. Unless directed by the customer otherwise, use the means in which the customer contacted you to follow-up. If the person includes other data in addition to the primary means in which they contacted you use it. If they call and leave a home and work number, try both numbers to reach the customer. If they leave an email address, send a reply to the email with a hard copy of the reply in the mail. The idea here is that you want your customers to know that you are responsive. ■

#39

Close the Loop

After any customer service related call or customer complaint always take the time to close the loop. Follow-up with the customer to ensure everything is back to normal and their concerns have been addressed. Follow-up can come in the form of a telephone call, face-to-face visit, email, voice mail, or letter. This is often thought of as the "second effort" program.

Typically, you will want to wait a period of time to allow the customer to experience a change in service. A day, a week or even a month might pass. But be sure to close the loop. ■

#40

Personalizing Service

One of the most effective ways to show customers that you appreciate their commitment to your business is to use their NAME. Your name is the most important word in any language. The use of a name in the world of customer service is a sure way to show you are licensed to serve!

It may cost something to obtain a customer's name from a marketing standpoint, but once you have obtained a name, the effective use of it will pay dividends. Here are ways that names can be used effectively:

- ✓ Logging back onto a website and being welcomed back by name

- ✓ A call center representative who uses a customer's name effectively throughout an interaction

- ✓ A restaurant that prints a name on matches and trains its employees to use a customer's name throughout a dining experience

- ✓ An automobile service representative who uses your name before telling you about a $2,000 repair you need

- ✓ A hotel that provides overnight guests with preprinted business cards displaying their name and hotel address, phone and fax while they are "in residence"

- ✓ A hotel that programs your name onto your in-room television screen to welcome you back

- ✓ The pizza delivery business that uses your name once they have your phone number

✓ Once you learn someone's name in a face-to-face introduction, give the gift of interest by using their name throughout the interaction.

The television show CHEERS opens with this concept and sings its praises in the theme song, "Where everybody knows your name." Norm is a repeat customer who is greeted by name each and every time he walks in the door. What does it cost to use a customer's name? Not much, but it can cost you a customer not to use it!

A restaurant that deserves mentioning for doing a fabulous job using guest's names is Emeril's in Orlando. You know, Emeril "BAMM" Lagasse, the now famous television chef from Louisiana. If you are fortunate enough to get a reservation at his restaurant located in Universal Studio's City Walk, you expect the food to be special. And, it is – one of the best dining experiences ever! But the food is not the entire story. You see, Emeril also knows the importance of great service in his restaurant. From the time the greeter seated us until the wait staff said good night, our last name was used no less than six times in two hours. They make it their business to know your name and use it. The fabulous service and scrumptious food combined for a memorable evening that we hope to enjoy again in the future. Thanks Emeril! BAMM! ■

#41

Create a Captain's Table

Customers seem to get it right every time. They KNOW when they are dissatisfied. So what can you do to make certain they are satisfied? Look at service through your customer's eyes – not your own.

One way to do this is to contract with a shopping service that will provide a mystery shopper for you. This type of firm provides its clients with a written critique and scorecard of a shopper posing as a client. Often they will provide a cassette tape recording of a phone interaction. The tape makes for an outstanding coaching and counseling tool with an employee when critiquing the interaction.

Here's how a car dealership took a novel approach to obtaining customer feedback:

The service manager contracted with a group of taxi drivers to provide transportation for customers while their car was being serviced. The cab driver's job was to not only provide transportation, but to also find out how satisfied the customer was with the service at the dealership. As soon as they came across an unhappy customer, they called the service manager right away so the manager could follow-up as soon as possible to fix the situation if possible.

The question for you is – who are your taxi drivers? Who is out there getting feedback on the satisfaction level of your clients? Many customer service savvy firms employ a third party to gather client satisfaction data. Clients may be more open to speaking candidly to this third party, than someone employed by the business. This type of feedback is vital to client retention because the process focuses on the client's business, not yours.

Bottom line, if you are a manager, try not to have a cup of coffee alone. Pull customers together and share a cup of coffee. Think about the Captain's table on board a cruise ship. The purpose is for the Captain to say thank you for your business and listen to the passenger's feedback. ∎

#42

Break the Silence

Quiet customers don't necessarily mean happy customers. To ensure your quiet customers are indeed satisfied with your products and services you should take the initiative to break the silence to learn what they really think about your product or service. This can be done in the form of face-to-face, telephone, email/direct mail, or surveys.

One note of caution, if you're going to ask for problems, be ready to address them as they arise. Anticipate problems and have a recovery plan handy for each. ■

#43
━━━━

Take the Time to Track Your Timing

Time can be both a friend and enemy in customer service. Those who provide effective customer service are conscious of time in all aspects of the customer interaction:

✓ How many rings does it take for your customer service department to pick up the phone?

✓ Do you measure the average length of a customer service interaction?

✓ Do you keep metrics?

✓ How often do you put a customer on hold? How long?

✓ How long does it take you to solve the average customer problem?

✓ How fast can you solve the easy problems?

✓ How long does it take you to solve the difficult ones?

✓ How long does it take you to locate customer information?

Time can be your enemy if customers perceive that their time has been wasted. Or, time can be your friend if your prompt service and support saves your customers' time. The point is to be conscious of time. ■

YOUR MISSION

If you never stopped to measure time, you should. Begin to keep metrics or employ CRM (Customer Relationship Manager) software that will do it for you. Post the metrics in a place where employees can see and internalize them. Pick 2-3 to emphasize including one leading indicator (a prediction of future success) and one lagging indicator (a measurement of something that already happened).

#44

Real-Time Customer Service

Once a sales brochure or price sheet is printed, it's a dead document. Updating it may require reprinting the entire job, an often costly and time consuming process. The Internet has replaced a stagnant piece of information with real-time information that is alive – updated, corrected and instantly replaceable. This real-time information is available to both new and existing customers to view, print and use via your web site.

This concept not only applies to static information like instructions and brochures. Information in general – frequently asked questions, demonstrations, free trials, updates, price quotes on upgrades – can be real-time information.

This real-time approach to doing business and moving information on an individual and customized basis has revolutionized the way we interact with one another. Company web sites, online banking, bill paying, smart cards and electronic checks and debit cards are the ways we all will soon do business together. Make the Internet and your web site your literature depository. As you need brochures, fact sheets, pricing list, print them as you need them ■

YOUR MISSION

Are you prepared for this opportunity?

_____

_____

_____

Does your site offer the ability to send and receive email?

_____

_____

_____

Conduct a live chat session with a customer with a question?

_____

_____

_____

Don't be afraid of HTML. Learn how to upload and replace HTML files to provide greater customer response.

#45

The Art of Acknowledging and Addressing Problem

To acknowledge is to align with the customer's state of mind. It is not to agree, but to broadcast that you have an understanding of how the problem or situation is affecting him. That understanding can be based on your own similar experiences, others that you know who have had similar experiences, or experiences that you can only imagine. It is important that you align and acknowledge in proportion to the customer problem or challenge at hand. If the customer is frustrated due to a late delivery of a package from your company, you might acknowledge by saying something like, "I can understand how frustrating it is when you expect a delivery on a particular date and it doesn't arrive. Recently, I had a similar experience." However, if the person is upset because of a late delivery of a package, and let's say that package is a heart transplant, you just can't align from your own experience – unless you are a heart surgeon. In this case to align, you must imagine. You might say something like, "I can only imagine how difficult this situation must be."

Aligning or acknowledging doesn't solve the problem or even advance your customer service cause. It simply puts you on the same level as the customer for a sentence or two. This dialog translates into time. That time translates into an opportunity for you to connect on a personal level. If the customer believes you are genuine and that you understand his situation, even if you only can imagine it, he is less likely to be upset and more willing to move towards a next step and solution.

The sentence after the acknowledgement statement is one

that begins to turn the conversation towards a solution to the problem. It is the point at which you move the customer from negative to neutral or from neutral to positive. So, the second half of an alignment or acknowledgement statement is where you might say something like, "With your permission, I would like to put a trace on the package and see exactly where it is, OK?" or you might say, "Let me see what I can do to resolve this issue and get the package to you as soon as possible?"

Here's the progression: step one is to align; and step two is to move the conversation forward. One downfall of many poor customer service encounters is when the rep jumps immediately into step two. By jumping to the solution phase, the rep does not have a genuine understanding of the customer's situation. Consequently, the customer is more likely to cancel, become more frustrated or look to a competitive solution thinking you just don't appreciate the business or have a complete understanding of the problem.

How long do you align? It could be a moment – even a moment with no words spoken. In a face-to-face situation, sometimes just a sincere look of concern, a slow shaking of the head from side to side, or a look of pain when the customer tells his story is enough to relay to the customer that you "got it". A short verbal response of 'wow" or "that's not good" or "really" may be enough. The point is aligning can be done verbally or non-verbally depending on the situation and how much needs to be said can range from a single word or a page or two.

Remember that step two should always be a permission question to move to the next step. Making it a permission step allows the customer to feel that he is in control and helps him psychologically believe there is forward motion to the process. This allows the customer to feel that the call is productive and that his action has caused an event to happen.

We all tend to acknowledge or align, but usually only in the worst cases where it is just bad manners and insensitive not to do it. Try aligning as part of a one-two strategy and you will instantly see a change in your customers and yourself. This approach has you working together as a team to solve the problem rather than remaining in the roles of customer service rep and customer. I can understand your hesitation or reluctance to try this technique at first, however you will soon find it to be one of your most effective customer service weapons. Why not try it on your next customer who brings a problem to you? ∎

#46

Acknowledging the Customer's Need

A cknowledging the customer's need builds on the skill of acknowledgement, but has a strategic purpose embedded into it. The purpose is to genuinely find out what the customer wants or desires as an outcome. Rather than just assuming the outcome or customer desire, you confirm it. When a customer says, "You're late, it was supposed to be here by 10 AM and it isn't. I want my money refunded and I want to know where the package is at this moment!"

You might respond by saying, "As we speak I am making a note to refund the cost of the package. Furthermore, if you wouldn't mind staying on the phone with me, I will trace the package and get you a location. Will that meet your needs?" ∎

#47

■

The Importance of Empathy

Often times we tend to think of customers as an entity. Anyone providing customer service must empathize and identify with customers on an individual basis. Customers like to feel that their problem or situation is unique, and consequently, the solution is, too.

For example:

I was having a good flow and easy exchange of information with a FedEx tracking person via telephone. There was no hostility in either one of our voices, just a simple tracking question on an international shipment. After the woman confirmed the tracking number she said to me, "All I need now is your patience while I search for your package." I thought to myself, since you politely asked for my patience, no problem, you've got it now! This is a simple, but powerful illustration in the area of customer service. The FedEx telephone agent showed empathy towards me because I was about to be placed on hold . . . and who knows for how long! Have patience with me . . .

This story is in stark contrast to the story Roger Dow of Marriott International likes to tell his audiences about a missing suitcase. A passenger was berating an airline employee at the missing luggage office of an airline. As the passenger's face reddened and voice got louder, the airline employee was overheard saying, "Sir, there are only two people in the world who care about your missing luggage and one of them is losing interest quickly!"

Your ability to empathize with the customer is an important trait of a good customer service rep. Like acknowledging or aligning, it helps broadcast to the customer your understanding of the impact the problem has on the customer. Empathy on the other hand is not sympathy. Don't apologize or feel sorry for the customer. Empathy is understanding through their eyes. It is your ability to put yourself in the other person's shoes for a moment.

Don't dwell too much on the empathy. Look for verbal and non-verbal signals that let you know when to move on to the solution phase of the customer service process. A word, a sentence or at most a paragraph is enough to show empathy. More than this, and it will probably not appear as genuine. Too much empathy and you'll come off as phony and destroy the trust needed in a good customer service relationship. ■

YOUR MISSION

How can you instill empathy in dialog, scripted responses or actions?

#48

Hire For Talent - Train for Skill

If you think you hire people and then "teach" them how to provide customer service, think again! Providing customer service is a both a talent and a skill. Skilled employees think with empathy, show discernment, care, and in general behave in an outgoing manner. It's your job to identify natural talents and enhance them through training.

How do you hire for talent when interviewing for customer service positions? It can be as simple as:

✓ Prepare the right questions to ask

✓ Ask them

✓ Sit back and listen effectively

The right questions to ask are those which tap into their experience at handling situations. Called "behavior-based questions," they will start off like this:

✓ Tell me about a time when you had a customer complain to you about delivery time of a product

✓ Tell me about a time when you worked effectively under pressure

✓ Tell me about a time when you had a customer who said they were unhappy with a product

✓ Tell me about how you handled a difficult situation with a co-worker

✓ Tell me about a time when a friend told you they needed help in finding a job

✓ Tell me about a time when you were forced to make an unpopular decision

✓ Tell me how you've dealt with a very irate customer

✓ Tell me about a time when . . ask something important to your specific business

What you are listening for is "did the person personally provide help or did they refer or attempt to avoid the situation all together." You want to hire a candidate who can deliver a great performance, not just talk a good game.

Ask a series of these behavior type questions to get a number of real life examples of how the person behaves in situations. This will give you keen insight to the heart of a person's natural talents.

One further thought – people have a difficult time "making up" fictitious answers to behavior type questions because you are asking them to tell you their story. The answers you will get are much more insightful than asking a traditional question such as "What would you do if you encountered a customer with a problem?"

Asking that type of question opens the door to an answer that anyone can give such as . . . go out of the way to help, ask what they need, etc. But, the difference is – they have never done it!

For example, Mike Hirsh, my college professor, often used to ask this question in an interview: Tell me about one of the funniest things that ever happened to you. The answer would reveal at least two things: 1) can the person think on their feet and tell a story; 2) can the person laugh at themselves when they were the brunt of a joke or funny situation. His opinion was that in the restaurant business, you need to be able to laugh at yourself quite a bit or the pressure could eat you alive! ■

YOUR MISSION

For your particular business, make a list of 5 behavior-based questions you would ask of an applicant. At the same time, be thinking about the types of answers or key words you would be listening for in a good response from an applicant.

#49

On-the-Job Training Versus Off-the-Job Training

Upon being hired as a front desk clerk at a newly opened Stouffers Hotel in Arlington, VA, the desk manager said to me, "In order for you to be successful at the desk, you need to be trained prior to working on the desk." The important role that effective training plays in customer service cannot be overstated. If an organization believes in customer service at the very top, then each and every person who interacts with customers needs to be effectively trained. One way to sum up a company's commitment to training might be – "Behaviors reflect values." Or more clearly "actions speak louder than words."

My first week of work, I reported at 3:00 PM to a room with a cash register, training manuals and lots of simulated questions and answers. For the first five days, three hours daily, all I did was work in that room with a manager learning what was expected from me. At 6:00 PM, I was off duty to complete homework, but did not report to the front desk. My second week on the job was my first experience working on the desk. I "hit the ground running" as they say. No trainee nametag for me. From the first minute I interacted with customers on the desk, I knew what was expected of me. I felt very good giving directions to guests, checking people in, etc., because I wanted to do a good job. Most new employees want to do good work.

One of the most important roles of a manager is to give all employees the knowledge and tools necessary to be successful on the job. This gets back to the point of behaviors reflecting values. If an organization expects employees to deliver outstanding customer service, then they need to model it themselves and set employees up for success! ■

YOUR MISSION

What job training do you offer?

_____

_____

_____

What can you do to simulate the real work environment?

_____

_____

_____

How might you use technology to make this process more efficient?

_____

_____

_____

How do you determine someone has completed training?

_____

_____

_____

What objective measures do you have in place for the above questions.

_____

_____

_____

#50
━━━

Anticipate Customer Service Needs

In a service environment you should always anticipate customer needs. This means doing your homework and creating knowledge or physical materials that can be used immediately to handle inquiries or problems. An excellent source for this type of information are frequently asked questions which should be captured and standard responses created for the customer service representative to use. Once captured, be sure to group them by their affinity to one another. Develop these materials for the customer service representative to use, as well as materials for the customer to access via mail, fax, email or website. Your application:

✓ Provide one sheets that offer a scripted response, suggested phrases, steps or procedures to use in conversation. Example: how to handle a billing error.

✓ Provide faxable one sheets that outline specific steps or procedures for the customer to follow. Example: how to handle directions to a nearby restaurant.

✓ Provide predrafted emails that can be further customized on the fly. Example: things to do in the area.

Also if you know that a service problem exists, acknowledge it on a recording that the customer receives first. (Many cable companies use this technique when service goes down.) Let the customer know you are aware of it and the steps being taken to solve the problem. It is better to use this proactive approach rather than allow the customer to stay on hold only to inform you of a problem you already know about. ■

#51

Look for People Doing Things Right

Managers are quick to find fault in their employees and place blame. Instead of focusing on errors, try a different approach and seek out and reward people doing things right. When you see a customer service rep do something good, reward the employee in front of their peers. State specifically what you liked about what the person did and offer some type of reward, even if just words of praise. Even receiving a sincere round of applause during a staff meeting from fellow employees will be remembered by the employee and the behavior is sure to be repeated.

If you don't have time to recognize people doing things right, hire a shopping service that can do this for you. ∎

#52

——

Customer Service to a Diverse Population

If you held a ball in your hand that was black on one side and white on the other and asked two people standing on opposite sides of the ball what color they see – one would say black and the other would say white. Technically, they would both be correct, but only partially accurate. You see, two people can look at the same object and see different things. Until the two people looking at the ball change positions with each other so they can see what the other person sees, they are biased because of their own view of the ball.

This same bias can apply to the way that people with cultural differences view customer service. Think about how diverse the population is that you serve. How many different ways can you come up with to categorize people or groups of people? A partial list could include:

✓ People of color

✓ Caucasians

✓ Different ethnic groups

✓ Gays/Lesbians

✓ Women

✓ Men

✓ Young children/teens

✓ Age in general

✓ Physical disability/mental disability

- ✓ Religious beliefs
- ✓ Occupation/Unemployed
- ✓ Married/Divorced
- ✓ Education level achieved
- ✓ Children at home/None
- ✓ Language
- ✓ Dress
- ✓ Wealth/Accent

Admittedly, this is just a partial list! When you think about delivering service to people or groups of people from the list above, it can be overwhelming.

There are a few points to keep in mind when you are thinking about the way in which you and others deliver customer service to such a diverse population. First, people are not always accustomed to your normal policies and procedures. This means that whenever you find your self having to explain something to a customer, try to put yourself in their shoes. Remember, the example of the two-colored ball. Picture yourself trading places with the person on the other side. Second, many of us talk too fast. Slow down when speaking, especially if there is a language barrier between you. Third, if there is a written policy or sign, refer to it when explaining yourself. Lastly, keep your frustration under control. You're not the only one who may be feeling this way. Show empathy by imagining what it feels like to be in their shoes.

Here is an overall guiding principle that may help you when serving customers:

Try to focus on the situation, issue or behavior – not the person.

This is much simpler to say than it is to do. But this principle will force you to make better decisions by looking at the bigger picture and not just at the individual. It will also help you consider others' points of view, not just your own.

A tip to remember is this – whether on the phone or face-to-face with a customer – put a smile in your voice or on your face at all times because a smile is universally understood as meaning "I care!" ■

YOUR MISSION

Does your particular business deal with a diverse customer base? If so, you and your group of employees may want to attempt to act out the following role-plays. You may certainly customize each scenario to your industry or operation. Experience also tells us that people learn when observing how NOT to handle a situation effectively. You might want to instruct people to first role-play what NOT to do before demonstrating the best method.

✓ Explain a change in policy or procedure to someone who is much older.

✓ Approach a parent to explain their child is misbehaving and not following the rules.

✓ Explain whom to serve first when a man and woman approach you at the same time that are not together and a telephone is ringing that you are responsible for answering.

✓ Discuss your refund policy to someone who speaks very little English.

✓ Listen and explain your delivery policy to a person on the telephone who is upset and thinks the product is already late.

#53

International Service – The Disney Way

When you travel outside the United States, it does not take long to understand that even though it's a small world people do deliver service differently around the globe. One of the ultimate customer service challenges would have to be the Olympic Games. Bringing visitors together from around the globe for two weeks is a huge undertaking when you think about it from a servicing point of view. Now think about it from a daily standpoint at the Disney theme parks. Every day must be like hosting the Olympic Games!

Diversity plays a key role in understanding multicultural differences. Disney draws creativity from diversity and it is a core competency for the company. When Disney opened Epcot Center, it brought together the cultures of eleven different countries. Each of the pavilions is staffed with international representatives, many of whom have participated in Disney's Multicultural Ambassador Program, which fosters multicultural education and understanding and helps people discover the resources in themselves and others. Young people travel from their native country and participate in a year-long experience. It is Disney's version of the Olympic Village where people live with as many as five other people from different countries.

The program focuses on three key areas:

✓ how Disney interacts with its guests

✓ how it attracts and retains a diverse work force

✓ how it celebrates multiculturalism in the local community

We certainly realize that not all organizations can put the same resources as Disney does towards serving its international clients and customers, but perhaps their Ambassador Program will spur an idea for your situation. One thing that Disney understands is . . . the visitors they attract daily do prove it IS a small world after all. ∎

YOUR MISSION

Consider the following to define your international customer service plan:

✓ What percent of your client base can be truly called International?

✓ Have your employees been through any type of diversity training?

✓ Do you believe you could improve the way you provide service to your international clients?

✓ What resources are available to you? For example, internal company training programs, any internal employees with a strong background in dealing with diversity issues, external training through a company, local colleges/university programs, non-competing firms in your area that attract and serve international clients.

✓ What would the return on investment look like for your organization if you put resources towards improving customer service to the international market?

✓ Learn to say hello, goodbye and thank you in the languages of those you commonly serve.

✓ Visit www.icsa.com to learn more about the International Customer Service Association. It contains a wealth of good information.

#54

—

Understanding X-Gen Employees

Can generation X employees provide good service? Yes, they can! But many of them have not personally experienced good customer service. Remember people born after 1971 have not driven up to a gas station and had someone come out and fill up their car, wash the windows and check the oil.

In the X-gen world, they have shopped, bought clothes and done their homework in front of a computer monitor – not with a person. To them, customer service is an "experiential" thing, not a theory. They cannot often relate or get turned on to a great customer service story because they can't relate to it. It is something they have to feel. And once they feel it, they begin to learn how to give it back!

When you have a done a good job at hiring for talent, X-Geners will provide good customer service IF IT ENHANCES THEIR WORLD – not ours. It is the principle of WIIIFT — What Is In It For Them. And it is not just money.

✓ What motivates the younger generations you work with?

✓ What does respect mean to them?

✓ How do you prefer to be communicated with? How do they?

Armed with these answers, you will be on the way to a relationship with that X-gen employee (or most employees for that matter) that is built on understanding and trust. When you are in a position that uses your natural talents, the job becomes fun and rewarding. The X-genner then realizes that they are enhancing their place in the world. ■

#55

Customer Service and Kids

If the products or services you sell in any way involve kids, don't forget to capture their opinions too. In a restaurant don't just ask the adults if the meal is OK, but direct a question directly to the child. Even ask the child if he could add something to the menu what would it be? Or if they could make the items on the menu differently how would they do it.

If you include a customer response card with your product or service, include one for the adults and another for the kids. You may be surprised to find out how the reasons for purchase and the features and benefits desired differ greatly.

When it comes to food, kids can be very difficult customers to please. Do it right and the kids will often lead the parents back to your place of business again and again. My 10-year-old son, like many, just doesn't eat a wide variety of foods. But put him in front of a Sizzler kids buffet and he's in heaven. The buffet is just his height, and the items on the buffet are things that he likes – everything from macaroni and cheese to gummy worms. Now kids are not the neatest bunch – so if a buffet bar isn't an option create a virtual one. Laminate pictures of various items and allow the child to circle with a crayon or grease pencil those items he or she would like to see on their plate. Invest in kids plates that have compartments for those who don't like to have their food items touch. Allow the child to pick three or four items to complete their virtual buffet.

A balloon, a little toy, or anything that will make a child feel special goes a long way to maintaining their happiness and keep their parents coming back. McDonalds and other fast food chains know the power of prizes and kids meals. How many times has your child begged to go to one of these places only to not eat the food but just play with the fifty-cent toy. Go to you local dollar store and look for little gifts that would make a child happy. ■

#56

Handling Returns

People hate making returns for something they've bought because they may encounter long lines, complex return policies, lost receipts and slow help. Most stores are designed to get goods out of the store, not to return them. Frequently, you'll see twenty registers to check out and one to check in or make returns.

How do you handle returns? Is it an easy process? Do you make your customers stand in long lines that trail out the front door? Do they have to fill out their life story and provide all types of ID? Bottom line: it should be as easy to return an item as it is to buy it.

How can you make this experience more enjoyable? Provide:

✓ A flyer to read

✓ Free coffee

✓ Store coupons

✓ Post a sign that says, "We appreciate your business!"

✓ Note times when the returns line is at its smallest

✓ Give customers the ability to put the item down, give them a number and allow them to shop. Call them when it's their turn or on deck.

For any employee, handling returns is not fun. To improve the experience have very well trained people on this job and consider paying a premium to these employees. Also try to staff up so that there is always an extra person working near by. Train managers to jump in when the line grows long. ■

#57

Under Promise and Over Deliver

The phrase, under promise and over deliver, is often easier said than done. When customer expectations are set so high by sales staff or others in a position to set them, you may set a standard that is difficult to meet. This is where teamwork comes into play between your selling staff and customer service team. Often, a salesperson will set very high expectations to earn the sale. In some cases making claims or promises that will be difficult to keep. Consequently, when the product or service is delivered and the expectations are not met, a gap exists. Typically that gap is translated into a call to the customer service department or worse, a cancelled order.

For example:

As the manager of a consultant team, I had one consultant on the team who continued to get poor reviews specifically around the question that the course did not meet expectations. Since we all taught the same course to similar audiences, I decided to observe the trainer in action. Within the first 10 minutes of the seminar the problem became apparent. He introduced himself and the program. No problem so far. Then he went on to talk about the course. He was obviously enthusiastic and knowledgeable about the program. He went on to tell the audience it was the highest rated program of its kind, 450 of the Fortune 500 companies use it, and it will do more for their careers than any program. Do you see the problem?

The consultant created such high expectations that when participants were going through the course they were waiting for some life altering moment, and of course that moment never came. As a result, at the end of the program their expectations were not met – not because the program did not meet the objectives set forth by the seminar materials – but because of the amended objectives the seminar leader had added.

After the session I provided feedback to the instructor. I simply said next the time you deliver this program simply state the objectives as they are printed in the leader's guide. Do not elaborate; don't spoil the opportunity for the participants to have their own "aha" experience. The consultant followed my instructions and was happy to report that his participant scores were back on track. Program expectations were not only being met but also exceeded.

Customer service reps have a unique perspective due to the fact that they know the problems that can arise with a particular product or service. They also know what extras, benefits or freebies that they or the sales team can use to save a sale or account. If you give them all away up front, you have no surprise to give back in the end.

If you promise happy and deliver elated – you are a customer service god. If you promise elation and deliver only happiness – you may be history. When was the last time you raved to your friends and neighbors about a company, product or service that only met 70% of your expectations? Under promise and over deliver and you will have a lot of happy – no, make that elated customers. ■

#58

───

Disarm the Chronic Complainer

Every customer service rep has one: the chronic complainer. You can tell just by the way the phone rings that a chronic complainer is on the other end of the line. There will always be certain customers that you just cannot please no matter what you do. Experienced customer service representatives know how to avoid falling into the chronic complainer's trap by disarming the complainer before he creates a situation that you believe is hopeless.

The secret is to get the customer involved in the solution. Now I realize that many of you may not be in a position to allow a customer to create his own terms. So to remedy this you might say:

"NO PROMISES Mr. Customer, but if you could, what solution would you propose to make you happy and ensure your continued use of our product?"

All of the sudden the customer is in the virtual driver's seat with no promises attached. Make sure you are clear upfront that there are no promises. Sometimes I even say it twice or seek a confirmation from the customer that we are only playing "what if." Assuming the customer presents a solution that is feasible for your company, before jumping in and saying you'll do it – you must confirm. *Is there anything else? What you're saying is if this and that happen then you will be satisfied, correct?* The reason you ask twice is to prevent the customer from coming back and asking for more. I have seen too many people apply this technique only to give away the farm because they forget to ask twice. Use the whole technique – not just half. After all, how can a customer argue with himself. ■

#59

When a Major Problem Occurs...
Conduct a Post Mortem

When something does go wrong with a big account, you should do a post mortem. Ask the customer to explain what went wrong, when, why, and how. Think of it as an autopsy. Not only will you learn from this investigation, but the customer will appreciate the honesty and professionalism associated with the act even if he is no longer a customer.

However, if you do a post mortem, make sure you also implement a plan to prevent the same problem from happening again based on this new insight.

Some companies will even go as far as to create a post mortem specialist. This special examiner, a senior customer service rep, reviews the situation and, if necessary, contacts the customer to draft a formal report. The information is then formatted in a variety of ways: one version is provided for the customer's review and files, another goes to the customer service team for coaching and feedback, a third goes to senior management to make them aware of any systems or policy problems, and a fourth is entered into a knowledge database for historical, benchmarking and trend purposes. ∎

#60
———

Phonetiquette—First Impressions

It may seem like an obvious thing to do if you are in business, but you would be surprised how many times it may not happen. Develop a plan that designates an employee to pick up the phone on the first or second ring. Have a back-up person at all times who will pick up the phone in 3 or more rings. Having a consistent voice for your business is important.

Call your place of business and pretend you are a customer asking questions. Which employee handles you the best? Which has the best phone manners and etiquette? Who is able to answer your questions most effectively? Which person would you want to do business with today? ■

YOUR MISSION

What can you do to coach employees who answer the phone?

_____

_____

_____

- ✓ Create a job aid for commonly asked questions.
- ✓ During slow periods have your reps cold call one another. Ask various questions and provide the answers with feedback on their response.

#61
___

Create a Menu of Options

G ood customer service reps always have the ability to offer their customers a menu of customer service options. When working out a customer problem, the customer should not feel like the customer service rep is making up solutions on the spot. The customer will feel more secure if they believe that a process with specific options and remedies exist. If they perceive the process is one that can be negotiated, it opens the door for long, protracted and customized-solutions on a customer-by-customer basis. ■

YOUR MISSION

Think about the common customer relations issues you face on a daily basis. What options exist to remedy these customer problems? Do the remedies you offer vary by customer service rep? Do the remedies offered vary by time of month, customer size, product, or other variable? Are the remedies consistent across product lines or across account service reps? Execute this on a grid.

Creating a set menu of customer service options creates consistency in your offering. You might further divide the menu options into three columns. Those columns might include initial remedy offered to customer, remedy offered to customer if they continue to complain, and supervisor-only authorized remedies. You could also divide the three columns into small customers, medium customers and large customers usually dollar volume or order volume as a column heading.

Provide this internal tool to your customer service team. Furthermore, metrics can be obtained by reps as to the remedy most often used.

#62

Up Selling

U p selling is best described when you go to McDonalds and after placing your order having the counter person respond saying would you like fries with that? When done right, it can be extremely effective – but it can also become obvious and almost a cliché when done wrong or when it is overused.

When a customer makes a purchase, up selling simply is the process of either adding to the purchase or in some cases upgrading the customer to next higher model (and price range). If the person buys a VCR you may ask if he would like some blank videotapes to go with it. If purchasing a new DVD player, suggest a wild special effects movie that will clearly demonstrate the power of the DVD to his friends and family.

Up selling is the ability to raise the average of what each customer spends in your store by 10, 20 or 30%. Think about it, you could go out and try to increase sales by 30% or you could just employ up selling to do the same thing with your existing customer base. What if you did both? Up selling comes in the form of extended warranties, installation services, home delivery, overnight delivery, design services, additional product, or anything that personalizes the experience for the customer. ■

YOUR MISSION

What products or services can you upsell?

_____

_____

#63

___

Gratuity in Advance Concept

Everyone knows that a gratuity is a tip for service. A good gratuity normally means a thank you for the good service that was delivered. A poor gratuity usually reflects on the poor service someone has received. If you follow the line of thinking that a gratuity is a form of acknowledgement for service, consider this novel approach:

Give a gratuity in advance to ensure good service!

This doesn't mean tipping a maitre d' for a good table or tipping a waitress in advance of your meal, although you could do that if you chose to. Here is its application in business:

When a large group brings a convention into a hotel for a meeting, they can literally take over a hotel. As one might imagine, it takes a tremendous amount of coordination to successfully orchestrate the servicing of hundreds or thousands of customers. One particular association, GMDC (General Merchandise Distributors Council) met annually at the Marriott Resort on Marco Island, Florida. Their meeting planner, Bill Wheeler, believed that the resort staff played a significant role in the overall success of his convention. He would do two specific things prior to the start of his convention each year that made his group stand out in the eyes of the Marriott staff.

On the night before the large group would arrive, Bill and his staff would invite three to four key members of the resort management team to go to dinner. He would also insist that the managers bring their spouse or significant other to dinner as well. At some point during dinner, Bill would propose a toast. In his toast, he would tell the spouses of the managers that he really appreciated them because over the next few days, they might not be seeing much of their husband or wife because GMDC would really need them. I can remember waking up the next morning after dinner and my wife saying, "You better get out of bed and get to work because Bill is there waiting for you!" She wouldn't say that about other groups!

The second thing Bill would do was to personally visit the key departments throughout the resort and leave boxes of chocolates and other goodies the day before his group would actually arrive. It was his way of saying, thank you in advance for all the hard work done on behalf of his group over the next few days.

Bill's philosophy on customer service was that the Marriott staff was really an extension of their association staff during the convention. He wanted his members to feel very special and receive outstanding customer service. As Bill says, "If one message gets lost by an operator, it is a reflection on us as an association staff for selecting this place. I figured let the staff know in advance how much I appreciate their work and maybe they'll go the extra mile for our members and us."

The gratuity in advance concept worked. GMDC came back year after year and it was the Marriott staff's favorite convention to work – because they felt appreciated – in advance! ∎

#64

Seek Out and Understand New Technology

Today, more than ever before, new technology is helping us create and maintain customer service relationships. Web meetings that include live chat and web video conferencing today are affordable and easily accessible by anyone with an Internet connection. Email is an effective means to send company newsletters, surveys, promotions, and any other form of communication to your customers. Company web sites today can include frequently asked questions, product and service feature and benefit guides, interactive tutorials, and examples of product and service applications. Accessibility to your customers and your customers to you is now available via wireless technologies. Today, there really is no excuse not to respond immediately to a customer call for help. Customer service today and going forward has because a 24/7 – 365 environment.

Customer relationship databases, management programs, tracking programs, and other electronic means in which to better communicate and serve your customers abound.

Customer service should be factored into your company voice mail, email, newsletters, website, brochures, and any other form of communication you have with your customer.

Here's an example for the real estate industry. I came across a very creative way to provide outstanding client service 24 hours a day — the "Talking House." When a prospect drives up to your home, a yard sign encourages people to tune into 1610 AM on their radio dial. Prospects then hear the listing agent describe all the features that make this house special. The radio signal comes from a small transmitter inside the property. The "Talking House" is marketed out of Fond du Lac WI by Radio Technologies – http://www.talkinghouse.com.

One of the most convenient technology tools is literally at your fingertips: a database. This type of program can help you track customer communication and plan when points of contact should occur. Use it to remind you to: send a card on a customer's birthday; call the customer 30 days prior to a contract or service plan expiration; remind a customer at regular intervals to change their oil, rotate tires, service their furnace or air conditioner. The database organizes your action list so all you have to do it follow it. ■

#65

━━

Interior & Exterior Appearance

Did you ever walk into a store and just by the look of it walk out? Have you ever had doubts about whether or not the store could indeed deliver the products or services as advertised? While there are always exceptions to this rule, the point to remember is that the appearance of your work area visually speaks for you. If your customer service location is in an area visible to customers, make sure the area is neat, clean and professional. Loose papers, dust, stacks of files, old furniture, or walls that look like they need a coat of paint can influence the customer's impression of you and your company.

A poor environment and the image it presents should not be left up to the customer service representatives, but should be controlled by management. Create standards. Reward positive behavior and those who keep neat desks. As a last resort, put up a wall so you can limit what the customer can see or hear.

Interior Checklist

✓ Poor lighting also affects customers. Consider upgrading the wattage in light bulbs in the ceiling or adding additional fixtures

✓ Open or close the drapes depending on the view

✓ Paint using corporate colors

✓ Re-carpet heavy traffic areas

✓ Replace bad ceiling tiles

✓ Clean fingerprints off glass, displays and monitors

✓ Dust equipment, computers, and displays

These are all factors that influence first impressions.

Exterior Checklist:

In addition, look at the entrance to your building. Customers can form an opinion even before entering your place of business and speaking to you.

✓ Do you see potholes in the parking lot?

✓ Are there fingerprints on the entrance door, or cigarette butts or trash on the ground?

✓ Do you hear squeaks?

✓ Are any signs broken? Do you have appropriate signage? Do you have parking lot signage? Is there signage that easily points the customer to your office or store front?

✓ How is the lighting at night?

✓ Are trash recepticals available, clean and emptied on a regular basis?

It only takes a minute to make an impression – make it a good one. ■

Who is Responsible for Customer Service

Now that you've been introduced to over 60 ways to incorporate *Optimum Customer Service* into your business, take it to the next level with a greater understanding of how to create a *culture of customer service* within the hearts and minds of all levels of employees. The following chapters will address:

Customer Service Defined

Departmental Commitments

Attitude of Service

Psychology & Traits of the Super Customer Service Person

Customer Service Philosophy & Plan

Customer Service Defined

I t is vital that everyone involved in a business understands the impact of customer service in their daily interactions with customers. Here is a framework to build *optimum customer service.*

✓ *Who gives customer service?* Everyone in the company – owner, CSR, sales rep, receptionist, cashier, driver, etc.

✓ *Who gets customer service?* Every customer and prospect, as well as internal customers — your fellow employees.

✓ *When do you deliver customer service?* At every customer touch point.

✓ *How do you deliver customer service?* Through the words you say, the tone and actions in which you say them, the posture you take when speaking, and through the written or spoken word of the marketing and advertising messages and images used.

✓ *What is customer service?* A consultative environment where the customer feels and thinks that his or her questions or concerns are genuinely understood and proven by the answer or information offered.

✓ *Why provide customer service?* Customer service is necessary to gain and retain customers. Customer service generates good will. The more good will a customer has towards your company, the more likely that customer will continue to use, seek out and stick with your company when a customer service moment occurs. Bottom line: customer service differentiates you from your competition. It moves customers from merely satisfied to extremely satisfied.

✓ *What is a customer service moment of truth?* A customer service moment occurs when there is contact between you and your customer. That contact can be direct or indirect, face-to-face, electronic, or through the printed word. It is the moment when a customer asks a question or expects a response from you or the product or service you represent. For example: quickly offering a mutually acceptable solution to a problem; or, assisting a customer by comparing the features and uses of a piece of equipment which saves time and reduces confusion and frustration.

Just as an audience congratulates a performer with applause, your customers applaud customer service with repeat business and recommendations to others. A company's bottom line profits can be measured by the applause from customers due to outstanding performance or service delivery.

Departmental Commitments

Customer service is affected when departments work well together and when they do not. The objective of *departmental commitments* is to create an environment of departmental cooperation through advance planning, written commitment, performance, ratings, peer pressure and recognition. Here is a procedure to create this internal support.

Department heads meet at the start of each month. Each department prepares a written scope of the 3 or 4 most important projects/issues they are going to undertake over the next year. These projects/issues should be big enough in scope to have a positive impact on customer satisfaction, employee satisfaction, P&L, or sales. Progress would be measured every 30 days.

At the meeting, each department head explains the project/issue and asks for the commitments needed from other departments over the next thirty days to make progress or gain closure.

The department head who owns the project/issue obtains a signature of commitment from the other department head(s) they need. It should be understood in writing the resources and timelines that are being agreed to.

At the end of each month, the department head who owns the project/issue rates the other departments on a scale of 0 (no commitment) to 10 (total commitment) on the basis of how well the other department(s) lived up to their written commitment.

Finally, scores are turned in and plotted on a spreadsheet.

These scores are tabulated for the month and factored into an average for a year-to-date score on each department. These scores are then posted in an area that employees can see. This process applies monthly pressure to improve the individual departmental cooperation and scores.

At a glance, a manager can learn which departments are working well together and those that are not. To further motivate employees, incentives can be company-wide or department-specific. This rating can be factored into a manager's annual performance evaluation or bonus.

Attitude of Service

T ruly effective customer service reps have an innate *attitude of service*. What is it? *It is a true and genuine willingness and desire to serve others.* Examples are everywhere from the flight attendant who loves her job, to the friendly telephone service rep who speaks to you 1000 miles away from a call center, or the waiter who fills your water glass without having to ask or presents you with a fork if you drop one, or the check-out person who offers you a coupon at check-out for a sale item. You know these people. How? Because they stand out from the crowd. They make your customer experience memorable and enjoyable. These are the folks that you leave a little extra for when you tip. These are the folks who pick up the phone even if store hours are over to answer a question. These are the folks who you call by name even after just meeting them for a minute. These are the folks you look for when you revisit the store or call back. Why? Because of their attitude of service. Nordstrom's department store has made a name for itself by creating a building full of people like this. This is the way they do business. It is not the exception – it is the norm and it is expected.

A person who has an *attitude of service* is pro-active and not reactive. This person takes initiative and doesn't wait for something to go wrong before acting. This person has a system to contact you and checks how you are doing before a problem arises. This person treats you in a way that makes you feel like family. Bottom line: someone with an *attitude of service* does what is right, and if there is a decision to make he or she tends to always make the right one.

There are many ways to project an *attitude of service*:

Sincerity

Good customer service representatives are sincere. Their analysis and opinions offered around the customer service problem are honest and true. They become an advocate for the customer on a mission to find a mutually acceptable solution – one that is acceptable to both the customer and the company.

Manners

The use of manners may be common sense, but is rarely common practice. Those with an *attitude of service* integrate basic manners into daily conversation and interactions with customers:

✓ Use please and thank you

✓ Greet a customer using Mr. or Ms. and the person's last name

✓ Open the door for customers or prospective customers

✓ Offer to get them something

✓ Use *may I, pardon me* and other words and phrases that show courtesy

You want to project yourself as a professional, not an amateur. It is the professional who can say the right thing at the right time. The amateur wings it and is not conscious of the words he uses during a customer service interaction. A professional constructs his phrases with care and purpose.

Compliment Freely

When a customer is using your product or service, take a moment to pay a compliment. A simple statement like:

✓ "You look great in that."

✓ "That car looks great on you."

✓ "That suit makes you look younger (or older)."

✓ "That pen in your hand says power."

✓ "Thank you for choosing our product."

You cannot over use "thank you" when speaking to your customers. It can be applied to every aspect of a customer conversation whether positive or negative:

✓ Thank the customer for calling

✓ Thank the customer for bringing a problem to your attention

✓ Thank the customer for his patience or understanding

✓ Thank the customer for her cooperation

✓ Thank the customer for holding

There is a reason "thank you" is known as a magic word – use it.

YOUR MISSION

Consider your *attitude of service:*

How do you project an attitude of service to your customers?

_____

_____

_____

How do you answer the phone?

_____

_____

_____

How do you train your people to project an *attitude of service?*

_____

_____

_____

What active things can you do to project an *attitude of service?*

_____

_____

_____

What passive things can you do to project an *attitude of service* such as policies, displays, voice mail greetings, website messages, etc.

_____

_____

_____

Psychology & Traits of the Super Customer Service Person

What ingredients make someone effective and successful in providing optimum customer service? No one can say for sure, but there are some characteristics and traits that help this person shine:

✓ sharp, honed and polished

✓ prepared for change

✓ a good listener

✓ a natural smiler

✓ excellent interpersonal skills

✓ possess total product knowledge

✓ empathetic to the customer's needs

✓ positive in attitude

✓ prepared for any objection

✓ familiar with the competition

✓ willing and able to adapt her presentation on the fly and shift gears at a moment's notice

✓ always has the company's interest in mind, but at the same time can identify with the customer's needs

✓ upbeat

✓ a superman

✓ a politician

✓ ethical

✓ consultative

✓ not easily ruffled by irate customers

YOUR MISSION

Survey a few of your good customers, by asking some of the following questions:

What personal characteristics do you like best in customer service representatives?

_____

_____

_____

What if anything separates our company's brand of customer service? (Hint: If the answer is nothing...you have work to do.)

_____

_____

_____

On a scale of 1 to 10, with 10 being the highest, how would you rate the attitude of our customer service reps?

_____

_____

_____

Customer Service Philosophy & Plan

very customer leaves satisfied enough to want to return!
This is one of my favorite mission statements! Simple,
service-related and applicable to everyone. What is your
customer service philosophy? At a minimum you should have a
statement that summarizes your belief on the treatment of
customers. The former Philadelphia Marriott Hotel's mission
statement was "To provide an environment of complete guest
satisfaction through personalized service in a quality facility."

The mission statement should be a general rule of thumb. It
should be posted for all customer service people to see. All
employees should be aware of it, especially those in sales.
Depending on how customer service-centric you are, you may
also want to post it in a place where your customers will see
it.

As a general rule, the more your business is service-related,
the more important a customer service mission statement is
and the more likely you should have it prominently displayed.
Many companies will even wrap entire marketing promotions
around it or make it the defining characteristic of their
business, allowing them to differentiate themselves from the
competition.

Keep it simple. If you conduct a new-hire orientation, the
mission statement can be explained and supported with any
other training materials. It should be brief enough so that it
can be remembered and recited by employees.

Do you have a formal employee guide to customer service?
At a minimum, you should have a mission statement that

supports your customer service philosophy.

What type of training do you provide your employees prior to them interacting with customers? At a minimum, you should have a job aid that provides the employee with insights on the suggested way you would like the customer to be treated. In other words, there should be consistency with the customer service you offer and it should not be a variable depending on which customer service representative interfaces with the customer. A tabbed notebook is the easiest way to orientate employees on how to handle particular situations or problems. Electronic computer-based systems are also available for those businesses that need them.

YOUR MISSION

Consider the following to define your *Customer Service Philosophy:*

✓ Is the customer always right?

_____

_____

_____

✓ Do you fix problems?

_____

_____

_____

✓ When do customers have it their way?

_____

_____

_____

Here are some questions to help develop your customer service plan:

What is your current customer service strategic plan?

_____

_____

_____

Do you wait for the customer to call or visit with a problem, and then do your best to solve it?

_____

_____

_____

Do you track your problems?

_____

_____

_____

Are you proactive versus reactive in your approach?

_____

_____

_____

Do you have a special number customers can call (toll free) or a special section of your store where customers can make returns or address their concerns?

_____

_____

_____

Do you allow anyone to interface with unhappy customers or do you have a designated customer service savvy person?

_____

_____

_____

How many times do you allow the phone to ring before answering it?

_____

_____

_____

Do you place people on hold? If so, for how long?

_____

_____

_____

What is your average hold time? Is your average hold time getting shorter or longer over the last year? How many people hang up after being placed on hold? Do you track that number?

_____

_____

_____

Do you offer music on hold? Do you offer advertising messages on hold?

_____

_____

_____

Do you provide an opportunity for customers to leave a detailed message and then have a rep get back to them rather than being placed on hold?

_____

_____

Do you notify the holder the average or expected hold time?

_____

Do you allow the caller any automated self-service options such as getting account balances or store hour information or directions to the store?

_____

Do you track and maintain a ratio of number of sales to number of customer service calls? Again, is that number getting better or worse over time?

_____

Do you make a second effort to follow-up calls to ensure satisfaction?

_____

The products or services that may require customer service are:

_____

The customer obtains customer service by...

_____

_____

_____

The employees who handle customer service are..

_____

_____

_____

They are trained by...(computer program, online, book, role play, on-site training)

_____

_____

_____

If the customer wants to speak to a manager or is dissatisfied with the customer service, the process that follows is...

_____

_____

_____

Returns of products or services are handled how?

_____

_____

_____

Determining Customer Service Touch Points

Successful organizations today understand that it is not a question of high-tech or high-touch; the issue is combining high-tech with high-touch! It is fine to use technology to help streamline efficiencies and discover root causes of problems, but it is people who play the pivotal role of providing high-touch personalized service. This section will address the tools to determine customer *touch points* – a defining moment of customer service – by using the survey tool, needs analysis, questions, and observations. The goal of this section is to help you understand the customer's perspective of the service/sale interaction. The following chapters will address:

Touch Point Questionnaire

Established Benchmarks

Obtrusive Customer Service Metrics

Unobtrusive Customer Service Metrics

Lagging Indicators

Customer Service Blind Spots

Reduce Opportunities for Error

Quality as a Feature

Consumers as Test Subjects

Working Your Past Customers

Informal and Formal Customer Feedback

AOL Customer Service Survey

Touch Point Questionnaire

A "Touch Point" is a defining moment of customer service. Think of a defining moment or recent story from your organization as it relates to customer service. This is an opportunity to learn from your experience. Take the time to answer the following questions and share them with others. The Reference Section in the Appendix features case studies on how fellow business leaders proactively used these questions and answers to strive for optimum customer service.

YOUR MISSION

✓ What did the organization learn from it?

_____

_____

_____

✓ How do you do business differently as a result of it?

_____

_____

_____

✓ What customer service measurement methods are used against the different external (and internal) audiences you serve?

_____

_____

✓ How are the results shared?

_____

_____

_____

✓ If you could improve one thing about your customer service function, what would it be?

_____

_____

_____

✓ What stops you from doing it?

_____

_____

_____

✓ If you could "brand" your customer service, what would be the defining characteristics of the brand?

_____

_____

_____

✓ What would the brand "look like" from the customer's perspective?

_____

_____

_____

✓ What is one thing your competition does better than you in the area of customer service?

_____

_____

_____

Established Benchmarks

If you haven't done so already, you should begin to measure key metrics associated with the sales and customer service of your products and services. Too often we hear business owners and managers saying they had a good month or a bad month, or that this month was worse than last month – all subjective measures.

Noted Total Quality Management (TQM) consultant Dr. W. Edwards Deming once said, "If you can't measure it, you can't manage it." A benchmark allows you to spot trends and objectively measure whether or not you are doing better or worse as a result of your efforts. Benchmarks can be daily, weekly, monthly, quarterly, or annually. Any one measurement that may appear out of range with those that proceeded it must be examined and placed into the context of past months' results. Such benchmarking when graphed will allow you to create forecasts and anticipate success or failure in any given area of your business that you choose to measure.

Good customer service benchmarks include:

✓ number of purchases

✓ number of returns

✓ number of phone rings

✓ average time per customer service interaction

✓ average cost of remedy

✓ reason #1 why people called

✓ reason #2 why people called

✓ reason #3 why people called

✓ the number of times the manager intervened or was needed

YOUR MISSION

✓ What benchmarks can you track and measure in your organization?

_____

_____

_____

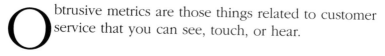

Obtrusive Customer Service Metrics

Obtrusive metrics are those things related to customer service that you can see, touch, or hear.

✓ How many customer complaints do you receive each month?

✓ How many returns?

✓ How often does the phone ring at your place of business?

✓ At what times?

✓ What kinds of questions do people ask most?

✓ How often is the person answering the phone able to provide answers to the caller?

All of the above are examples of obtrusive measures. In your place of business what can you measure? What can you see, touch, or hear that is customer service related? Pick those items you think will have the greatest impact on customer satisfaction and begin to measure them. Look for trends. Are they going up, down, or staying flat? Employ various marketing programs or shift policies and procedures to see the impact on the metrics.

YOUR MISSION

Identify obtrusive metrics and measure them over one month. Do you see any weekly trends?

_____

_____

_____

Unobtrusive Customer Service Metrics

Unobtrusive customer service metrics are those things that you cannot readily see, touch, or hear. They require analysis — usually of numbers or data that has been previously collected. Looking over your inventory records, what are the top 10 things you sell at your store? What are the 10 things you sell least? If most people buy particular items, what items can you place next to them that might spur additional sales? Think of it like putting the jelly next to the peanut butter or the limes next to the Corona beer. Little switches like this can double sales in very short periods of time.

Which check-out aisles are most people likely to use? Look at the floor. If you have been in business for a while it is possible that the floor tiles are noticeably worn in one lane than others? A quick way to get a fix on traffic patterns is to place masking tape on the floor. Over time the tape will wear more quickly in high traffic patterns than those less traveled. Depending on the amount of traffic, you can begin to see patterns emerge in as little as 24 hours.

If you are closed on Sundays, take a Sunday and park where you have a view of your storefront. See if anyone visits and what you can learn from the vehicle they drive or the way they act when they see you are closed. The same holds true if you close at 6 PM. Hangout near your door from 6 PM to 8 PM and note the people who try to do business with you after hours. How many people showed up? Would it pay to stay open past 6 PM? Maybe a drop slot would offer the customer an option to drop work off and pick it up tomorrow. A drop box is a way that you can remain open for drop offs 24 hours a day, seven days a week.

Bottom line — look beyond the obvious measures to those measures that are unobtrusive which may be invaluable.

YOUR MISSION

✓ What unobtrusive measure could apply to your business?

_____

_____

_____

DETERMINING CUSTOMER SERVICE TOUCH POINTS

Lagging Indicators

A lagging indicator is usually a number or statistic that highlights a problem or opportunity. Lagging means it occurs after a point in time. For example, the amount of customer service calls generated by a particular product or service could be a lagging indicator. In this case, a lagging indicator shows that a problems exists in the product or service. Unless you track the types of customer service calls you get, you may never link the lagging indicator to process improvements.

Other lagging indicators include: online hits to a website especially around customer service issues; or, the volume of calls to a phone number tracked by time and day of the week regarding customer service issues.

For example, you notice there has been a large number of calls due to a broken part. One approach is to simply replace the part and continue on with business as usual. However, getting to the root cause of the customer service problem, you begin to probe. You find that customers, when assembling the product, are putting the part on backwards causing it to break. Once you understand the cause you can develop a solution. One might be to clarify the directions, making them much easier to understand using graphics and pictures. But what about those who do not read directions? You decide the best course of action is first to begin shipping the product with that particular part pre-assembled. And second, to make a design change in the part itself. You redesign the part so that it can only be inserted the correct way, thus eliminating any opportunity for error. In this case, both a short-term fix and a long-term fix were identified.

YOUR MISSION

✓ Are you tracking lagging indicators? How?

_____

_____

_____

✓ What problem(s) did the indicator uncover and how did you resolve it?

_____

_____

_____

Customer Service Blind Spots

Many times your customer base begins to erode without your knowledge. To ensure you are not blind-sided by a variety of factors that may affect your customer sales and retention, you should regularly ask yourself the following questions:

✓ How many customers bought from you last month?

✓ How many were first time customers?

✓ How many bought within their regular buying pattern?

✓ How many bought outside of their regular buying pattern?

✓ If outside of their buying pattern, how far did they deviate, and why?

✓ How many customers stopped buying from you last month and why?

✓ What customer service reports do you regularly review?

✓ Which of those reports, if any, show patterns or are visual in nature such as graphs, charts, etc.?

Of the metrics you measure, what percentage are leading indicators (predict or forecast) and what percentage are lagging (past history, historical) indicators?

YOUR MISSION

✓ Identify blind spots can you identify from customer interactions? Are these lagging indicators?

_____

_____

_____

Reduce Opportunities for Error

Successful quality-oriented companies push towards defect reduction. The reason for this push is the tremendous competitive advantage it provides companies over their competitors. This is not an overnight process, and it is a tremendous commitment of time, money and behavioral changes. Those who adopt the process will reap the rewards.

The best example of defect reduction in action is the Japanese auto industry. In part, it is based on Dr. W. Edwards Deming's "14 Points of Quality" where vital processes were benchmarked. Then the process is engineered and continuously re-engineered with the goal of continuous improvement.

While the quality concept and defect reduction have been reserved for the manufacturing sectors, it is spreading to service-based organizations. Firms like Motorola, General Electric, Florida Power & Light, Ford, Cadillac, Citigroup, and Federal Express are all operating in this quality environment. Why? Fewer errors, defects and mistakes lead to greater productivity, increased customer satisfaction and higher revenue.

Think of defect reduction as the measurement of failures, defects, or bad customer experiences. Most successful companies average about a 7% defect/error rate. In other words, seven out of every 100 experiences you have with a company may result in defects, failures, or dissatisfaction.

A 7% defect rate would be disastrous for industries like the airlines, drinking water, drug prescriptions, and food manufacturers/packagers. As you can see, some industries must operate at a reduced defect rate (less than 7%) capacity for them to survive and maintain customer trust. Most companies not dealing with life or death situations – and not actively measuring defects – can survive at 93% success rate. The ideal rate, of course, is 100% perfection. However, the cost of moving from 93% to 100% grows exponentially as you approach 100%. Consequently, every industry has a "trust" point or "acceptance" defect rate.

Opportunities for error is a term borrowed from the quality movement. Bottom line, the more touch points there are in a process the more opportunities for error exist. An *opportunity for error* is a moment in time where what is expected or desired to happen, may not. If a customer is upset about your product or service not functioning correctly, you may want to inspect the item and measure opportunities for error. If 10 customers in a row return the same item due to a switch that does not work, odds are there is a defective switch in many of the similar units you sell. To reduce the opportunity for error, you may decide before selling any more items of this type to test the switch prior to sale. This approach will not only make your customers happy, but it will also eliminate the time and effort spent on handling returns.

Look at the sales and customer service provided to your customers as a process. Flow chart it on a piece of paper and note all decisions or points where the process may branch. Look for wait or idle times where either the customer or product stands idle. Look for opportunities to streamline the process. Look for opportunities to reduce or eliminate wait times and reduce hand-off and decision points. For each decision point that you remove, you decrease your opportunity for error. Think of your customer service as a process and commit to continuous process improvement.

YOUR MISSION

What kinds of opportunities for error can you control? Think about how orders are completed, how paperwork is processed.

_____

_____

_____

What opportunities for error can occur internally with fellow co-workers? Think about problems that have occurred in the past.

_____

_____

_____

What errors do you deal with that may be preventable?

_____

_____

_____

How can you adjust your processes to reduce opportunities for error?

_____

_____

_____

Can you reduce the number of touch points it takes to get the product from you to your customer?

_____

_____

_____

Instead of creating departments of people, can you cross train so an employee can handle the customer from beginning to end as opposed to handing the customer off from department to department?

_____

_____

_____

Can you outsource manufacturing, delivery, or other services to firms and only accept and pay for product in return that is defect free?

_____

_____

_____

DETERMINING CUSTOMER SERVICE TOUCH POINTS

Quality as a Feature

What happens when companies start to apply the defect reduction concept to their non-life or death products and services to enhance customer satisfaction and reliability? The company that can deliver quality (99.7% success) will have a tremendous competitive advantage over the company who is offering an error rate even just a few points less. The concept of quality as a whole will become a measure – a feature – used to position a product or service over the competitor's. For example, it will be an "our quality or defect rate is better than theirs" kind of comparison. This percent of defects concept will become so embedded into our culture that customers will begin to ask for it, incorporate it into business agreements and do business with only those willing to use such exacting measurements.

Consequently, knowing that many U.S. companies are quietly becoming quality-oriented, you must ask yourself what your firm is doing to reduce defects and improve its quality for its customers?

As mentioned, this is not an overnight improvement. It can take years and millions of dollars of reinvestment in a company to make it happen. Even more so, one way many companies will catch up on their quality is to outsource manufacturing, delivery and services to firms that have already embedded a quality ethic and statistical measurement process. After all, it will be less expensive in the long run to outsource work that can be performed at 99.7% accuracy, than pay for the in-house mistakes and rework of an accuracy rate of 93% or less.

Consumers as Test Subjects

One component of your customer service plan should always include customers as test subjects. Prior to launching any new product, soliciting information from your prospective audience is invaluable. The test can be informal or formal. An information test may involve giving customers free samples of the product and either obtaining their opinions verbally or in writing. More formal tests can be done in the form of focus groups, in-depth surveys, or trial product testing/installation.

Testing is a tool that you can use to determine whether or not you want to offer a product or service for sale to your customers. Excess inventory, wholesale returns and deep-discounted sales are signs that a company did not product test prior to sale.

Often times people will debate as to which of two strategies or promotion to use when marketing to new customers. The correct answer to this question is to use both and to measure each on its effectiveness. Studies show that a good promotion can be 58 times more effective than a bad one. It is in your best interest to continually refine and test your customer marketing strategies to ensure you maximize effectiveness.

One of the most effective ways to use test subjects is in a focus group. It provides you with the opportunity to take the pulse of your customer base around a particular topic, product, or service. A focus group typically consists of 8 to 15 people who represent the population you want to poll. For instance, they can be prospective customers if you want to measure what would make them buy from you. They could be existing customers if you want to measure your current product offerings. And, they could represent past customers in the event you want to find out why some customers decided not to do business with you again.

The following criteria are used to host a beneficial focus group:

Time & Place

A focus group can be held on the company premises or at a local hotel or conference center. Choose a hotel or conference center if you fear your building might influence their responses positively or negatively (unless you want to gain insight about your place of business). A focus group can range in time from an hour to a full day.

Questions

Take time to carefully phrase the questions you want to ask to ensure the data you collect is useful. Make sure the questions are clear and the response insightful. Ideally, ask questions that quantify how often, how many, etc. Ask open ended questions to encourage a free and open response. Who, what, when, where and why type questions are better than did, does, do, and are type questions. The latter will get you one word responses whereas the former will get you sentences or paragraph type answers.

Capture the Data

Determine how you want to capture the data. Often focus group sessions are recorded on audio or videotape. If you are recording, make sure people know they are being recorded. To prevent any last minute awkward moments, note that the session will be recorded in the invitation. Do not wait until the start of a session to inform the customers of the recording.

Use a Facilitator

Have a facilitator present to pose the questions and shape the dialog that follows. The facilitator should manage the discussion so that one person's views do not dominate the conversation. If necessary, the facilitator may even have to speak to a dominant contributor and coach them when to respond. For example, if they tend to always jump in first, ask the dominant contributor to hold off until others have had a chance to speak.

Enhancements

You should have beverages and some type of finger foods available either during or after the session. Finally, each participant should be rewarded with a small gift for his or her effort. Typically something related to the conversation in the $5 to $25 range is an appropriate thank you. The gift also keeps the door open for any follow-up questions you may have after the meeting ends.

User Groups

Another way to obtain customer feedback is through a user group. By encouraging and forming user groups, you provide an opportunity to obtain true unbiased feedback about your products and services. You may find customers using your products in ways you never imagined. When customers are talking to other customers, they tend to open up and be very honest about their experiences.

Your role is to host the user group. You should monitor postings and only edit under extreme circumstances in the case of obscene or offensive material. Allow the customers to dialog and only jump in as the subject matter expert when a question goes unanswered, if the information posted by another user is incorrect, or when you genuinely have something to add to the conversation.

A user group is also a great tool to test market new ideas, conduct surveys and gain feedback about recent products, services or price changes. A survey can help measure the impact of a price increase, help identify key selling points of a new product, or identify ways to improve service.

YOUR MISSION

Define the following criteria to host a beneficial focus group:

time and place _____

questions_____

how to capture the data_____

selecting a facilitator_____

enhancements_____

Create a user group on the web.

_____

_____

_____

Create an in-person user group.

_____

_____

_____

Working Your Past Customers

Another important group of customers are those who have left you. Contact them and ask why they no longer do business with you. This will provide you with strategic information you need to know in order to fix your problem before it's too late.

You should rank the reasons why your customers left. By addressing the top one or two reasons, you can reduce the number of future customers you could lose in the future.

YOUR MISSION

Can you think of a few past customers you have not seen or spoken to for a while? List two or three below and a date to follow-up with them.

1._____ Date:_____

Result:

_____

_____

2._____ Date:_____

Result:

_____

_____

3._____ Date:_____

Result:

_____

_____

Informal and Formal Customer Feedback

When was the last time a company you do business with asked you to provide them with feedback? Not just a response card, although they are one means to ask for input, but genuinely asked in the form of a face-to-face question, phone call, or a formal survey? Companies genuinely concerned about service should begin with a benchmark of how their customers view the current status of service. How else can you improve, or for that matter, know what to improve if you don't ask your customers? That is why they call it CUSTOMER SERVICE. Good service should not be defined by you, but by your customers.

Informal

At the end of a call or customer interaction simply ask the customer, "Is there something we can do better or differently to make your experience with us better?" Most may say "no you're doing fine" – but you will be surprised just as many will provide feedback. Ask your representatives to note the responses and document them noting the customer's name and their comments. Hold a contest for the representative who submits the most comments.

Here are other questions to ask that can help you better understand your customers:

✓ How well are we delivering what we promise?

✓ How often do we do things right the first time?

✓ How often are we on time?

✓ How quick is our response to your request for service?

✓ When you need to contact us, how accessible are we?

✓ How polite and helpful have we been?

✓ How well do we speak your language?

✓ How much confidence do you place in our products and services?

✓ How does our desire to keep satisfied customers show?

✓ How have we tried to meet your special needs and requests?

✓ How would you rate the appearance of our people, products, facilities, and website?

✓ How would you rate the quality of the service you received?

✓ How does our service compare to our competitors?

✓ Would you recommend our company to others? Why?

✓ Would you buy from us again? Why?

Formal

You could create a formal survey by yourself or hire an outside survey firm. It can be done on paper or electronically. The options are endless. Just make sure your questions not only provide you with insight as to where you've been, but also give you good information about where you should be going. Use a Likert Scale (1 to 5) to quantify and analyze trends. Today, there are many third-party websites that specialize in surveys. For example: zoomerang.com; keysurvey.com; hostedsurvey.com; web-online-surveys.com; surveymonkey.com.

AOL Customer Service Survey

In our recent lifetime, very few companies have grown the way America Online has. In 2003, more than 25 million households rely on AOL as their Internet provider. At AOL, they take customer service very seriously. They employ 8,000 people at call centers around the globe. Recently, AOL had the opportunity to provide me with customer service. What follows is a fine-tuned example of how feedback was requested via an online survey on customer service.

Questions 1-5 require a yes or no answer. X represents the person that assisted the customer.

1. Was X the person who assisted you?

2. How would you rate the knowledge of X in handling your transaction? 1 Poor – 5 Outstanding

3. Please explain why you rated X the way you did on knowledge.

4. How would you rate the courtesy of X in handling your transaction?

5. Please explain why you rated X the way you did on courtesy.

Questions 3, 4, & 5 request that you be as specific as possible and limit your comments to X as they use this information for coaching and developmental purposes.

6. Was this the first time you contacted AOL about this particular problem?

7. Did X resolve your problem on this contact?

Questions 6 & 7 give the options yes, no, don't know.

8. Please tell us how much you agree with each of the following statements:

    X clearly understood my question or reason for contacting AOL.

    X met all my needs.

    I believe my interaction with X added value to my AOL membership.

    The length of time it took to reach a Customer Care Consultant was appropriate.

9. At the conclusion of the call, were you offered the opportunity to hear about some additional AOL member benefits?

10. If so, did you speak with a consultant at our AOL partner location?

11. The offer I received was for: AOL Long Distance; AOL Network; AOL Credit Alert; AOL Wireless Store.

12. Overall, how satisfied are you with the support you receive from AOL?

13. Would you be willing to recommend AOL to a friend?

14. Overall, how satisfied are you with your AOL membership?

15. Please share any comments you have regarding the support you receive from AOL.

16. Is there anything else you'd like us to know about your AOL experience?

As mentioned, AOL understands the importance of keeping customers as happy subscribers. Think about the purchase power of these happy customers. Online commerce is a $100 billion a year business. Seven years ago, the spending figure was zero!

What does the future hold for improving customer service as it relates to AOL? They are focused on a strategy of convergence – the seamless, wireless flow of information and entertainment through televisions, personal computers, cell phones, radios and related devices. The key rests with broadband coming into homes over the next ten years. AOL's online unit is working on an "integrated mailbox" which will link people's many voice mail boxes and e-mail accounts to one central location – accessed from their AOL account. Now that will be great customer service.

Maintaining an Environment of Optimum Customer Service

Knowing how to provide *optimum customer service* is just the beginning. Changing behavior to continually provide *optimum customer service* is the goal. This section will address how to create the momentum that fosters *optimum customer service* – from words and actions to techniques and strategies. Integral to making the transition to *optimum customer service* is the "change model" that illustrates the different points involved in maintaining this successful environment. The following chapters will address:

Implementing the Change Model

Seven Customer Referral Strategies

Loyalty Versus Commitment

Honor Existing Customers Before Seeking New Ones

Empower Your Employees

$1 for Every Good Idea & Suggestion

Improve Your Decision Making Skills

Creating a Personal Relationship

Birthday Greetings

Build Your Database and Exploit It

Responding to Customer Traits

Recruit Good Customer Service Reps

Understanding the Customer's Needs

How to Turn Objections into Opportunities

The Art of Asking Questions — an Open and Closed Case

Maintaining the Relationship

Upgrades and Enhancements

Implementing The Change Model

How do you go about instituting changes to your level of service? Consider the following change model. In order for change to effectively take hold in any organization, all of these components need to be in place:

CLEAR SHARED VISION

✚

CAPACITY TO CHANGE

✚

PRESSURE TO CHANGE

✚

ACTIONABLE FIRST STEPS

✚

INCENTIVE TO CHANGE

=

CHANGE

The Change Model is simple, but not easy. It is simple to understand, but not so easy to implement. On the next page, the graphic shows how the change model works. Each component of the change model is defined to show the cause and effect of each condition on the ultimate result.

CHANGE MODEL
These conditions must be in place for change to occur.

A Clear Shared Vision **+** Capacity for Change (skills & resources) **+** Pressure for Change **+** Actionable First Steps **+** Incentives **=** CHANGE

This is what happens when these conditions are NOT met.

⊘ **+** Capacity for Change (skills & resources) **+** Pressure for Change **+** Actionable First Steps **+** Incentives **=** FAST START THAT FIZZLES

A Clear Shared Vision **+** ⊘ **+** Pressure for Change **+** Actionable First Steps **+** Incentives **=** ANXIETY, FRUSTRATION

A Clear Shared Vision **+** Capacity for Change (skills & resources) **+** ⊘ **+** Actionable First Steps **+** Incentives **=** BOTTOM OF THE "IN BOX"

A Clear Shared Vision **+** Capacity for Change (skills & resources) **+** Pressure for Change **+** ⊘ **+** Incentives **=** FALSE, HAPHAZARD START

A Clear Shared Vision **+** Capacity for Change (skills & resources) **+** Pressure for Change **+** Actionable First Steps **+** ⊘ **=** SLOW, GRADUAL CHANGE

CLEAR SHARED VISION — To provide an environment of complete customer satisfaction through personalized service in a quality facility. Customer's intent to return to use our services will rate at a minimum of 98%.

CAPACITY TO CHANGE (SKILLS & RESOURCES) — Management will have access to the best equipment, appropriate inventory levels, staffing levels and training to operate at a level that meets budget guidelines and customer expectations.

PRESSURE TO CHANGE — Competition is remodeling and expanding service offerings and our revenues are flat to the previous year, which results in a budget deficit of 5%. Plans and actions are due in 30 days.

ACTIONABLE FIRST STEPS — Form a Customer Service Committee made up of management and hourly employee representatives. Committee to meet within 30 days and submit an overall plan including timelines and resources necessary to improve intent to return rating from its current 95% to 98%.

INCENTIVE TO CHANGE — Committee to submit plans outlining incentive program along with measurement goals for return on investment.

If all of these steps are adhered to, there is a good chance that change will take place in that operation. The problem is that often times, all the steps in the *Change Process* are not in place. As a matter of fact, here is what happens when a step is missing from the model:

- ✔ If everything is in place except a **CLEAR SHARED VISION** — fast start that fizzles out because enough people don't clearly understand the goals and vision.

- ✔ If everything is in place except the **CAPACITY TO CHANGE** — anxiety and frustration set in because people don't have access to the resources or skills they need to be successful.

- ✔ If everything is in place except **PRESSURE TO CHANGE**

— it sits in the bottom of people's in-box and gets buried by the new priorities of the day or week.

✔ If everything is in place except **ACTIONABLE FIRST STEPS** — a slow haphazard start sets in because people don't know where to begin or whom is in charge.

✔ If everything is in place except **INCENTIVE TO CHANGE** — slow, gradual change may occur because people are not feeling or seeing the results of their efforts.

If this Change Model makes sense to you, we encourage you to adapt it to your customer service efforts. Perhaps it might explain why a project or team is "stuck in the mud." Truly, all five components of the change model must be in place for change to occur in a timely and effective manner.

Seven Customer Referral Strategies

One of the rewards of good customer service are customer referrals. When you "wow" a customer, treat him nice, go beyond what it is expected, customers respond by referring their friends, family and even complete strangers. By developing a customer referral program you are creating a continuing source of customers. Referrals are the purest form of word-of-mouth advertising which is the most cost-effective advertising there is. When done right, you can create an army of marketing people ready and willing to tout the benefits of your product or service.

Here are seven strategies for gaining customer referrals:

1. Simply thank your customer for referring others to you. Just the fact you have a sign or a message somewhere that your customer can see that says – "Thank you for referring us to your family and friends" – plants this idea into their minds.

2. Post somewhere in your place of business or in mail you send to your customers the names (with the customer's permission of course) of those who refer customers to you. This type of referral works great if the referring person is a business or business owner. Plus, publicizing the referral is free advertising for the person's business. Find 10 or 20 business owners and you will see how quickly they consistently send you leads in exchange for a mention to your customers.

3. Offer "something" to your existing customers at the time of purchase for the names of three people they know who may be interested in your product or service. At a minimum you should require an address or phone number to make the lead valid. Also ask, "Why you think they would be interested

in my product or service?" The answer to this question will allow you to personalize the letter, include the right information, or be the basis for the start of a phone call.

4. Include the details of your customer referral program on a bill stuffer, postcard promotion, or sign near the register. Offer a monthly drawing for a prize – say a dinner for two and a movie or some of your products or services for free. Each time a customer refers a client (they don't have to buy, but they do need a complete address or phone number) they get their name placed in the drawing. Also, take a picture of yourself with the drawing winners at your place of business. Hang it in a public place with a caption that again explains how the program works. Also, send the photo in the form of a postcard promo out to all the drawing entrants and your existing customer base. They not only see the winner, but you promote more entries for the next monthly drawing and at the same time keep your name in front of all your customers and potential customers.

5. Anytime you are asked to donate a prize or gift to a local charity or good cause do so with the stipulation that an entry form be completed. Again, in exchange for what you donate, at a minimum get business cards, or a slip of paper with the person's name, address and phone number.

6. Seek out events that have the same demographic profiles of the customers you like to do business with and offer a door prize at their next event. To enter the door prize, again ask for a business card or have the entrants complete an entry slip that includes their name, address and phone number. Note on the slip that all information must be completed to win.

7. Feature a success story of the month. Review customer purchases and profile one that is the most unique, biggest, smallest, or features a particular product or service you are looking to advertise. Print the profile on a large postcard and send it to your customers. Include useful tips or information on the card that anyone can use. Print extras of the cards and use them as part of your overall marketing efforts.

Loyalty Versus Commitment

There was a time in the United States when customers were loyal to businesses. People would drive a Ford because their parents did. They would shop at Sears or JC Penney's for the same reason their parents did – they could count on the quality and service. Besides, there really wasn't that much competition to choose from. Today, the competitive landscape of choices and service has increased ten-fold. A shift has occurred among customers from loyalty towards commitment. This shift translates into "customers will be committed to your business as long as the service and quality meets their expectations." As soon as one of those slips or disappears, customers will leave you in a New York minute!

Think about it. Poor service in a restaurant? Vote with your feet and go down the block to another restaurant. Poor quality on a car repair? Vote with your gas pedal and head to another garage or dealership. Disappointed in the fulfillment of a catalogue order or the delivery of an on-line order? Vote with your phone or browser and send it back and change companies.

Loyalty programs are great for initially building and then maintaining a strong customer base. Simply put, a loyalty program rewards customers for doing business with you. Usually there is a reward or incentive associated with the loyalty program. Many offer the reward in the form of points equivalent to the number of dollars you spend. You can either redeem the points immediately or save them up for larger rewards. In addition to points earned for purchases, loyalty programs will offer a premium. Such behaviors might be purchasing a particular product or service, shopping on a particular day or at a particular time. Use of these programs will help you push business towards products you want to sell, or enhance business on certain days or times (i.e., during your slower days or times).

A loyalty program can be as simple as a business card you sign each time the customer purchases to a sophisticated electronic key tag system. With ten purchases, you get the eleventh for FREE. This is a common practice at hair cut shops and service businesses that specialize in one type of service. Grocery stores track purchases and accumulate points via the courtesy card. At checkout, you know points earned, points used, dollars saved on sale items, as well as coupons for other like purchases.

Bottom line – a loyalty program that is personalized, easy to use and redeem wins customers. All things being equal, customers prefer to shop where they are rewarded. It is this loyal customer behavior that is the product of a loyalty program. But, the customer will still try out a competitor if your service and quality do not meet their expectations.

Honor Existing Customers Before Seeking New Ones

Maintaining existing accounts is less expensive than investing in the marketing and acquisition of new accounts. Prior to soliciting new customers you may wish to review your existing customer database for those customers who are inactive or have cancelled accounts. Often a quick phone call or visit to the customer is enough to uncover why they have stopped doing business with you. Sometimes the customer forgot about you, sometimes a new decision maker is in place, it is possible that your newsletter or communication strategy only includes mailings to active customers versus inactive customers and you may need to revise this strategy.

In some cases, the customer stopped doing business with you due to a problem that was never resolved to the customer's satisfaction. Again, taking the time to find out exactly what went wrong and what it would take to win the customer's business back, is all that is needed to re-initialize the relationship.

YOUR MISSION

Look over your existing customer database and create a printout of all inactive and/or cancelled customers for the last few years. Assign that list to a particular customer service rep or sales person and ask him or her to follow-up with each of the customers.

Their Task: Position the call, acknowledging the fact that at one time the customer did do business with you and that the purpose of the call is to see what we can do better to win back your business.

You will be surprised how many of these calls will generate active customers.

_____

_____

_____

_____

_____

_____

Empower Your Employees

Empower every employee to become a customer service ambassador for your company. Any frontline employee should be trained in basic customer service skills and have the ability to handle customer service issues.

Who are these front line employees? For example, those who deal with customers in tough situations such as when an airline loses someone's luggage or a hotel front desk clerk who deals with a guest who was up all night due to noise in the next room. Whenever possible, prevent handoffs and empower the employee to make all decisions necessary to satisfy the customer.

YOUR MISSION

Who is your front line?

_____

_____

_____

Are they prepared?

_____

_____

_____

How would you rate his/her customer service skills?

_____

_____

_____

$1 for Every Good Idea and Suggestion

Any time a customer offers you a good idea or suggestion in which to improve your product or service, in addition to a thank you, you should send a letter in the mail and attach a crisp $1 bill. The dollar is a small token of appreciation which has high visual impact on the customer. Some companies make it a point to recognize the best suggestion of the year at their annual stockholder meeting.

YOUR MISSION

Think about five good ideas you've heard from customers. What are they? Now send your letters and $1 thank you.

1._____

2._____

3._____

4._____

5._____

Improve Your Decision Making Skills (PAAD)

Good decision making skills are among the best skills a customer service reps can possess because they are often tasked with making multiple decisions on a single call. Each decision is a fork in the road or a branch that may lead to another decision. A good rep will navigate through the decision making process to emerge with a successful resolution to the customer's problem.

Working with a formula or model will ensure that you treat problems, like people, with consistency and fairness. A formula is only effective if it is remembered and applied. One formula is Problem—Analysis—Alternatives—Decision or PAAD.

The first step is to define the problem: who what, why, when, and where questions will help you get the details.

The second step is to analyze. State or confirm with the customer what is occurring now and what is expected. Note the details on a notepad and refer to them as needed throughout the process. Once you understand the gap between what is occurring now and what is expected, confirm that your product, service or organization can fill the gap before moving to the next step. If not, do not move to the next step. If possible, suggest another path for the customer – to include, if necessary another solution.

The third step of PAAD is Alternatives. When developing your alternatives, begin with any "must" criteria. Must criteria are those things that the customer requests in order for an alternative to be considered. Try not to encourage must criteria. All other criteria fall into "want" criteria. These are criteria that the customers wants or would like to see as part of the solution. If an alternative fits so that both you and the customer can mutually agree on it, move to the last step: decision. If a single alternative does not work, don't be afraid to mix and match alternatives to find one that does. The fourth step, decision, is when you state the mutually acceptable decision.

Creating a Personal Relationship

Creating a relationship takes time – or better yet – instances. You might meet someone once and yet do business with them for years to come. Is this a true relationship? No, it is simply a business arrangement. Insurance people are good examples of this type of business relationship. Typically, you'll see them once and then just send a check from that point forward. At best you have phone contact – but odds are you will speak to the office staff – not the agent himself.

Look for "opportunities for instances." Six or seven instances of face-to-face contact whether over a month or a year begins to create a personal relationship. In the agent example, instance one might be a visit to the customer's home. Rather than mail the policy, create instance two and personally drop it off for signature at a time when the client would be home. Don't push for the signature, but create instance three when you follow-up a few days later to personally pick up the document. The client may even offer to drop it off. In this case, it provides an opportunity to see your office. Notify your staff anytime a customer walks in to interrupt you so you can take a moment to say hello and personally thank the person. A month or so into the policy create a fourth instance where you follow-up with the customer again in person or by phone to ensure satisfaction. Two or three months later, check in again perhaps with a birthday card to create a fifth instance. If you have a company party, invite select clients or look for ways to see them in public. If your town has a fair or some community event that most tend to visit, use this as an opportunity to meet and greet your customers. This type of chance meeting creates another instance.

The key point is the frequency of face-to-face, telephone and personal mail contact which creates a personal relationship.

Birthday Greetings

How many birthday cards do you get each year? Probably just a handful. Odds are sometime during your life, your dentist, chiropractor or insurance agent has sent you a birthday card. But unlike the card you get from your grandmother, there was never any cash gift inside. But, what can you give that has value? Perhaps a coupon, discount, or some other item of value that would have the same impact.

Don't skimp on the card. This is a reflection of you and your company. We all know that it is the thought that counts – but you don't want this image to cheapen your products or services by the card's appearance. Take a moment to write something personal and sign it. Also, hand address the envelope so that it looks like a card from friends and family. Omit the business cards, the impersonal pre-printed envelope and worse yet the preprinted signature. If you are going to invest in the card, envelope and stamp – invest the 30 seconds it takes to hand-write the envelope and sign it.

Build Your Database and Exploit It

What do you know about your customers? Do you know what they buy? How often? In what quantities? If given a customer's name, could you predict his next purchase from you? Do you fall into the trap of doing one size fits all marketing? Information is power – if used correctly. If you currently track your sales in a computer-based information system, a few modifications are all you need to start leveraging the power of information. Information to include are such things as:

✓ Customers first name and last name

✓ Business name

✓ Mailing address to include city, state and zip code

✓ Phone number

✓ Fax number

✓ Email address

✓ Company size

✓ Purchase history (days and hours you prefer to shop at this store)

✓ Occupation

✓ Birthday (just month and day)

✓ Customer notes

Obviously, you can include a variety of other variables, but the above should be the minimum fields in any database. Use the database as a means to effectively communicate with your customers. Using regular mail or email, send out newsletters, postcards, and other marketing materials designed to keep you and your company's name in front of your customers.

Each time the customer interacts with your company you should make a note in the customer notes section of the database. Especially if it pertains to future sales, customer service problems, or special circumstances when doing business with this customer. Other things to include in this area include personal information about the customer such as product preferences, where they went on vacation, birthdays, kids, names, hobbies and other items that can be used to stimulate small talk and further build the relationship.

In addition, have customer information printed on an index card to take advantage of an interaction. The customer can fill it out in a matter of minutes. At the end of the day just key the data into the computer. In addition to data offered, you may be able to extrapolate and include other information. Additional data would include miles from store (by entering address info and going to a site like Mapquest.com you can determine drive miles to your store.) If most of your customers come from work, you may wish to capture employer information on the card too. You may find patterns emerge among local area employers. You may want to track time of purchase, amount of purchase, date of purchase, and the list goes on and on.

Sophisticated retailers use this kind information and databases everyday. They create demographic (name, address, income, etc.) and psycho graphic (purchase decisions, what you buy) profiles and use these profiles to customize their marketing and promotion efforts. It is not one size fits all advertising, but a custom postcard with a custom promotion designed specifically for the type of products the customer likes to purchase.

A scattergram of where your customers live and work will also provide you with strategic information. Simply place a colored dot of ink on a map where each of your customers live and another color dot of ink in the area where your customers work. Look for patterns. What newspapers are they likely to read? At what store are they likely to shop? Visit which gas stations? Look for opportunities to cross market your products or services with other businesses in the area. Remember, the key to effective advertising is message and frequency. Put your name in front of your customers a few times a day and you have as much frequency as Coke or Pepsi.

Responding to Customer Traits

Your ability to read people and adapt your customer service style accordingly will take you a long way in creating satisfied customers. Some of the best service reps are those who can adapt to a variety of customers. They know how to connect, how to phrase words and sentences so they will most likely be accepted by the customer. Sometimes the same customer will go through a series of emotions during a single call requiring you to adapt minute by minute.

Here are some general customer traits and strategies to effectively interact with these types of customers.

The Driver/Decision Maker

✓ likes to be in control

✓ wants respect

✓ likes admiration

✓ serious, sometimes rigid thinking

✓ aggressive and demanding

✓ likes logic

✓ interested in end results

✓ organized

How to handle:

✓ let her do the talking, run the call

✓ ask direct questions

✓ compliment him

✓ acknowledge her comments

✓ stick to the facts

✓ build a case

✓ talk in terms of end results

✓ stick to business

The Socializer

✓ wants to be liked

✓ friendly

✓ talkative

✓ likes recognition

✓ likes to associate with others

✓ shares personal stories

✓ good sense of humor

How to handle:

✓ build a relationship

✓ talk about the benefits to the group

✓ be friendly

✓ tell client-oriented stories

✓ share personal information about yourself

✓ build trust

✓ tell a funny joke

Mr./Ms. Play It Safe

✓ high safety needs

✓ doesn't like risk

✓ likes to think about it

✓ likes to get others' opinions

✓ indecisive

✓ passive in nature

How to handle:

✓ go slow with your presentation

✓ pause to assure complete understanding and comfort along the way

✓ stress the benefits that promote safety or minimal risk

✓ ask her questions she can agree with

The Politician

✓ wants to make everyone happy

✓ likes to negotiate

✓ will say yes but not mean it

✓ non-committal

✓ likes to play games

✓ keeps changing the deliverables

✓ not genuine

How to handle:

✓ define expectations and deliverables before talking price

✓ ask alternative choice type questions

✓ be careful of games

✓ make sure he is qualified before presenting

Recruit Good Customer Service Reps

One of the biggest competitive advantages you can have over your competition is the caliber of your customer service staff. Do you just hire anyone and put him or her through training? Do you look for certain skills? Do you use psychological profiles to ensure the person is a good fit with your product, customer service philosophy or corporate culture? Just because someone worked in customer service before should not automatically qualify him or her for a job in your business.

Always wear your recruiting hat because you never know where or when you'll come across someone with good customer service skills. When you do, simply ask permission to contact him or her, or put on a mailing list. Certain people have a natural aptitude for service. Some of the best customer service reps we've encountered started as waiters and waitresses. They understand that good service is rewarded; they don't have to learn it.

Recruiting is the first step. Maintaining a first string CSR team means having a second string of "A" players in the wings. Some firms follow a philosophy of managing out the bottom 10% of the customer service team on a regular basis, either quarterly or annually. In order to do this, you must have replacements ready to fill the empty places with new recruits.

Understanding the Customer's Needs

Remember, you are servicing while you are LISTENING! The use of effective questioning techniques that qualify problems has become a lost art! Preparing the right questions and using active listening skills coupled with PATIENCE is the key to proper qualifying. You will want to ask questions designed to reveal the customer's needs and problems.

When qualifying the problem, you are trying to answer four basic questions:

1. *Does a need exist for your services as a customer service rep?*

2. *Should the customer be talking to sales?*

3. *Is the problem even related to the product or service we support?*

4. *Are you talking to the right person or at least someone who has an understanding of the product and is in a position to make decisions about what to do next?*

Here is a trap to avoid – do not jump on the first hint of a need or problem and begin fixing the problem. It is very tempting to do that when you first hear someone describe a problem that you can fix. We can't stress this enough – you are selling while you are listening! The goal in qualifying is to discover and prioritize ALL the needs and problems BEFORE you attempt to help solve them. BE PATIENT!

At this stage, you are playing the role of a problem solver. You should not present solutions until at least one primary need has surfaced and have confirmed that no other primary needs exist.

To confirm that no additional primary needs exist you might ask an open probe like:

What else is not working?

Or, ask a closed probe like:

Many of our customers who used the product you are using now found _____ to be a problem – is it a problem for you?

Customers will often contact you when they have a need for your services. Listen for key words like:

✓ solution

✓ wish

✓ need

✓ looking for

✓ want

✓ interested in

✓ like

✓ important to me

You might also hear the following key phrases while listening to a customer. In essence, the customer is qualifying herself:

✓ The solution to my problem...

✓ What our company needs is...

✓ I want a way to...

✓ I would like to have...

✓ I wish there was a way to...

✓ I'm looking for...

✓ What is important to me is...

Sometimes when a customer contacts you, he already has a solution in mind and knows what he wants. Unfortunately, this is the exception and not the norm. Most customers tend to talk in terms of opportunities or problems.

By definition, an opportunity or problem is a customer's problem that your product or service can fix. Unlike customers' needs or solutions, opportunities are not clear-cut statements stating a desire to solve the problem at hand. Problems are most likely revealed in the form of negative statements or complaints about the customer's current situation.

Problems are also not revealed as a result of the customer using "key" words or phrases. While needs and solutions are expressed as a customer's want or desire to solve a problem, opportunities are everything else. Basically, if there's not a clear need for your product or service, then it should be treated as an opportunity.

YOUR MISSION

As you read the following statements, notice the difference between customer problems and customer needs. Put a "N" next to the statements you feel are needs and an "O" next to those you feel are opportunities. For this exercise, pretend the features and benefits of your product or service can satisfy the following needs and opportunities.

_____ My current car eats gas; it only gets 12 miles per gallon.

_____ I want a car that gets good gas mileage.

_____ Our current invoice is difficult to read.

_____ I need an invoice that is easy to read.

_____ I'm looking for a way to improve productivity.

_____ Currently productivity is down.

Here are some sample qualifying questions to use:

✓ *What is your objective?*

✓ *What problems are you experiencing?*

✓ *How are you handling those problems today?*

✓ *What has been your experience?*

✓ *Are you the decision-maker?*

✓ *What do you see as the solution?*

✓ *So you're looking for a way to....?*

✓ *What can you tell me about the success and failures of past vendors?*

How to Turn Objections into Opportunities

It is often said that the sale begins when the customer says "no." Up until that point you are merely a presenter or marketer of information. Getting the customer to move from "no" to "yes" is the skill of selling and good customer service.

Objections are part of the selling process you must learn to love. An objection occurs when a customer has serious doubts or questions about your product or service prior to purchase. How effectively you handle your customers' objections will determine the outcome of your service efforts.

The novice often looks down on objections and does his best to minimize or downplay them. He does this by telling the customer his concern is unwarranted, tries to change the subject, or answers a simple yes or no question with long and drawn-out explanations.

The successful customer service representative – or any employee – welcomes the objection and treats it with the respect that it deserves. If it is important for the customer to take time to ask the question, or express his concern over a feature or lack thereof, it is important for the service rep to ensure the customer gets the exact answer he or she is looking for – even if it means losing the sale or customer.

How to Handle Objections

Here is a step-by-step approach to effectively handle objections:

1. The first step is to make sure you understand the objection. Take a moment to clarify any vague customer comments such as "It is a matter of timing."

2. Never assume that you can read the customer's mind. The last thing you want to do is to assume understanding only to find out the customer is talking about something else.

3. Once you clarify and confirm the objection or think you have a complete understanding of it, you should then take the time to confirm it. While it may seem that this step is redundant, the strategy here is to get the customer to define exactly what the problem is so you can apply a customized solution. An example such as:

"So what you're saying Mr. Customer is...(restate the objection), is that right?"

The key here is to get the customer to agree with your understanding of the concern. More importantly, if the customer says "No, that's not it" you have an opportunity to again clarify exactly what the concern or question is.

If the customer's objection is in the form of a question, simply answer it with a question:

"Does it copy more than 50 pages a minute?"

Your response, *"Would you like it to copy more than 50 pages a minute?"*

In the above example, we know the product can copy faster than 50 pages a minute. But what if it couldn't? You should try to massage the objection into something you can handle through the use of a clarifying or confirming question. Such as:

"Does it copy 50 pages a minute?"

Your response, *"It sounds to me that it is important that you get your jobs done fast and on time, is that true?"*

Most likely the customer will agree to this type of statement. Clarifying questions are important because they show you were listening, and more importantly, that you are moving in the same direction as the customer.

If the objection is not based on a simple question, you should then probe to uncover any additional hidden objections. Do not fall into the trap of answering the objection only to have another and another arise. Handling objections this way is like trying to hold a big wet slippery fish with your bare hands; you may be able to do it, but it is not pretty and the chances of slipping away from you are great.

4. After you confirm and understand the objection, acknowledge it and probe for more concerns. You might say:

"I can understand your concern with (briefly state the customer's objection). It sounds like that is an important issue and one that I would like to address. In the best interest of time, before I respond, is there any other reason you feel our product wouldn't meet your needs?"

Wait for a response. If you get one, probe it. Understand it. Confirm it. Acknowledge it. And then, ask for another. Continue to do this until the customer has no more objections. After she says no, ask her one more time just to make sure. You will be surprised how many objections pop out just because you ask twice.

5. Finally, you may want to ask the following question as a way to test the buyer's true interest or to close the sale:

"So if we can effectively meet and exceed all of your concerns, do we have a deal?"

Think of this process as getting all your ducks in a row. This approach of asking for and tabling all objections allows you to reorder the objections to best suit your needs and ultimately make the strongest case for your product or service. You may want to put the hardest one last, or maybe first. You may find that you can combine two into one and handle them together. Bottom line: Getting objections out in the open allows you to plan and mentally prepare if even only for a minute or two.

If the objection is based on a feature or benefit that your product doesn't possess, say so. It's best to be frank and up front with a customer. If your customer feels at anytime that you are being evasive, you will lose trust for the entire call and probably the entire relationship. At the same time, if you answer honestly and state your reasons in a professional manner, you build customer trust. This is very important for anyone who represents a product or service that involves repeat sales, works in a fixed territory, or must interact with the same prospects over time.

The product you offer today may not work, but the one you offer tomorrow may. Conversely, the customer's need for your product or service may not exist today, but it may tomorrow. If you have built a relationship based on honesty and trust, your chances of future success are far greater.

Often the customer asks questions or raises objections that simply require you to provide more information even after you have provided her with a complete and detailed presentation. The key is to have a couple sources available to handle the more information request. Newspaper and magazine articles, testimonials or a copy of your guarantee or warranty are credible and convincing sources of information. Simply hand the printed document to the customer and let it speak for itself. If it is a long article or large document, pre-highlight or underline the key points you want the reader to evaluate. Also, be able to circle or highlight key points on the spot.

Sometimes the additional information you offer can be visual or verbal in nature such as an on-site demonstration. Remember, if the "I need more information" objection comes before your presentation, your verbal presentation may suffice. If the "I need more information" objection comes after your presentation, it is a good indicator that you need something other than words – something tangible – and a printed, third-party endorsement such as an independent news or magazine article is best.

Many times you can make the customer's objection to your product or service the reason to buy and turn the perceived drawback of your product or service into the selling benefit that makes the sale.

If the customer says, *"Yours is too heavy!"*

You might respond by saying:

"Well Mr. Customer, that is correct. We have the heaviest unit on the market today and that is by design. Studies show the number one reason for mechanical failures is vibration. The lighter the unit, the more vibration. True, it might cost a little extra to transport it, but wouldn't you rather have a unit that has a stellar reliability record and lasts years longer than one that is in the repair shop for mechanical repairs? Quite frankly, the added weight and quality that is built into our units is the top reason our customers purchase our unit over the competition's. Do you see how the additional weight actually makes for a better and more reliable product and works to your advantage?"

Remember, if the customer takes the time to ask a question or express an objection, you have the skills to handle it effectively and make it work for you rather than against you.

YOUR MISSION

List the 3-5 most common objections you have to handle concerning your product or service on the left side. To the right of the objection, write a statement that effectively handles the objection.

The Art of Asking Questions – an Open and Closed Case

In order for us to get customers talking, they usually need to be directed with questions. If you want to learn more about customers, you'll need to plan a series of questions. You probably know the two main types of questions or probes are "open" and "close-ended."

Open Probes

An open-ended probe is used to obtain additional information from the customer. It's characterized by a few key words that force the prospect to elaborate on her answers so you can learn more about her needs. The question will require more than a simple yes or no response. This allows you to maximize time and effectiveness of the sales call. It also helps you to clarify and confirm needs, identify potential opportunities for business, build relationships, and illustrate your professionalism, competence, and expertise.

An open-ended question usually starts off with the classic open probe words: who, what, where, why, when, how, tell. Such as:

✓ Tell me about your...

✓ How would you respond...

✓ How can we make sure...

✓ Why does your company...

✓ Tell me how the final decision...

✓ What is the difference between...

✓ What do you look for in choosing...

✓ What if I proposed...

✓ Tell me who in your organization...

Asking open-ended questions is the first step in rapport building. Open-ended questions get the customer talking and you listening and taking notes.

By getting the customer to open up, you allow him to reveal opportunity areas where your product or service may be of value. This background information allows you to custom fit a presentation using the customer's information rather than a generic, scripted one.

YOUR MISSION

Think of the typical customer you tend to work with. List at least two open-ended questions that you would like to ask during your next interaction:

1.

_____

_____

_____

2.

_____

_____

_____

Closed Probes

A close-ended probe is used to confirm customer information. Close-ended questions are also characterized by a few key words and are useful when obtaining or confirming specific information or knowledge. The classic close-ended probes start with: is, are, does, do, did, have, would.

It can usually be answered in a simple "yes" or "no" response:

✓ Would you agree...

✓ Is it fair to say...

✓ Have you spoken to...

✓ Did you know..

✓ Is it true that...

✓ So what you need is...

✓ Do you have...

✓ Does it matter...

✓ So what you are looking for is...

✓ Are you aware...

Unlike open probes that are rapport makers, closed probes are rapport breakers! Try to have a lively conversation with someone by only asking closed probes. What you end up with is an interrogation!

Have a balance of open and close-ended questions prepared. Ask more open than closed and listen carefully to the answers. You will be amazed what customers will tell you — if you'll just ask and listen!

YOUR MISSION

List two close-ended questions you would like to ask during your next customer interaction.

_____

_____

_____

Next to each key word, write a question that leads off with the word designed to uncover a need for your product or service:

Who

_____

_____

_____

What

_____

_____

_____

Maintaining the Relationship

Maintaining the relationship with the customer is up to you. While some customers will be one-time opportunities, most of them will be lifelong customers. It is up to you to distinguish between the two and begin the process of maintaining the relationship.

What follows are some techniques and strategies on how to easily and effectively maintain the relationship.

Direct Mail

Maintaining the relationship using direct mail is one of the easiest ways to keep your name in front of your customers. Obviously, you will need a mailing address for a program like this. You can either create the list from past customer history information or you can purchase a list sorted by a variety of variables. Some of the variables include customers who:

✓ live within a x-mile radius of your business

✓ family income

✓ education

✓ own a car

Postcard

Postcards are great advertising tools. They are inexpensive from both a printing and postage point of view. If you use colored paper, include a big easy-to-understand offer, include your business name, address, phone, and map of where you are – you're in business.

Inserts

Tip-in advertising is also effective. You can either print a flyer or postcard and have it tipped into your local newspaper or you can join others in a prepackage compilation of ads. You've seen these envelopes arrive at your door – usually filled with 25 to 100 coupon type advertisements for local, regional and national businesses. Great if you are the exclusive provider of the product or service – not so great if you're not. Also, your ad becomes one of many the customer has to choose from – assuming the envelope even gets opened.

Letters

Letters to the customer are best if they are kept to just a few paragraphs on a single page coupled with some kind of offer. Preprinted tickets, coupons, discounts or anything that it looks like it has value – even pictures of money help. Don't embed the offer to reduce any purchase by 20% into the middle of the letter. Place it on the face of the coupon in big letters that says "This coupon is worth up to $2,000. Redeem for a 20% discount on any purchase made prior to [date future]."

Track your advertising programs. Put different promotions in different mediums so based on sales and customer interest you can begin to gauge which form of advertising work best for you.

Email

Email marketing will continue to grow as an effective means of putting your information in front of the client. Based on your own experience with email marketing, the following guidelines should be followed.

Always get permission to send the email to the person you are sending it to. Even if you get permission, include in the first email how they can be removed from the list. Some customers are very picky about what they get via email. This technique is very effective at reaching very large numbers of people at little or no cost. Because of this many people email the world with their offers. The last thing you want to do is get all your customers mad at you.

NEVER sell your list or allow others to mail from it without your customer's permission.

Include the offer in the subject line so the reader can quickly determine whether or not he wants to read it. Many people fail to do this and use a summary phrase such as "A Special Office from ABC Company." This doesn't tell the specifics of the offer. In addition, if the customer read it once and was not interested, future emails with the same subject line will get deleted before ever being opened.

Upgrades and Enhancements

Since the introduction of software, the concept of the product upgrade has moved from years to days. The new business attitude is to get it out the door first and fix any "bugs" in the next release or through the concept of a "patch." Think of a "patch" as a band-aid or fix to the problem. This aggressive philosophy is a result of pressure from several sides: worldwide competition, first-to-market, market share, embedding strategies, and customer demand. The days of waiting until you have crossed every "t" and dotted every "i" are over – at least for those companies wishing to stay in front of their competitors.

In the software and computer business, upgrades are commonplace. In the auto industry, you have a base model to which you can add options or upgrades. This approach allows the customer to customize the product to his exact needs. This also keeps the cost of the base model low and competitive. The customer pays more for only those options of interest.

Customer growth is an essential ingredient of every business strategy. Without customer growth eventually your customer base will mature and begin to decline due to competition and changes in customer preferences. When customers no longer see your product as unique and essential, sales will begin to decline and your customer base will begin to fall. Therefore, it is important to continually re-examine customer needs, customer preferences, the competitive landscape, and the product itself.

A trip to any grocery store will offer you a valuable education in repositioning existing products that have been around for years that respond to the current needs of customers. Examples are everywhere: new improved, change box size, create individual units, resize product, repackage product, new logo, new name, new image, new application, new price.

YOUR MISSION

Could you significantly reduce the price of your product or service by creating a base model with an options pricing formula?

_____

_____

_____

What have you done to overcome the drawbacks or "bugs" associated with your product or service?

_____

_____

_____

Touch Point Questionnaires

CUSTOMER SERVICE TOUCH POINT ANALYSIS: Provided by Mike Gamble, President & CEO of Searchwide — Hospitality Recruitment Experts, www.searchwide.com

DEFINING MOMENT – Conducting a search for the CEO position of a major US convention and visitors bureau, we had interviewed and screened all the candidates. The search committee and we were sold on the top prospect. I felt we had covered all the bases and had the right candidate nailed down. At the 11th hour, just before the final vote, the attorney for the bureau entered the room and revealed that his office discovered that the top candidate had been charged with a lawsuit for misappropriation of funds. That moment changed our lives for good!

LESSON LEARNED – Even though the attorney said that Searchwide did perform their job well and that we would have not have been able to uncover this information on our own, we learned that thorough background checks on all candidates are essential.

DO BUSINESS DIFFERENTLY – Now all candidates that are presented to a search committee have an extensive background check performed, no matter how long a relationship the candidate might have with my staff or me.

MEASURE CUSTOMER SERVICE – After a search is complete, I will contact 2 to 3 key members of the search committee to see how the search process was performed from their point of view. In particular, I key in on what could have been done differently to have made the process smoother. A few months after the new person is in the position, we will also contact key stakeholders in the community to discuss the new person's progress. There are times when a call to a stakeholder can be a source of new business for us.

RESULTS SHARED – I will share the results of my conversations on conference calls with the staff. Admittedly, this valuable information needs to be better documented for future reference.

IMPROVE ONE THING – SLOW DOWN! We are so quick to think that speed is the most essential aspect of a search. In fact, the opposite can be true sometimes. Even though people do appreciate how quickly we are able to fill a position, open time can be a valuable learning time for a staff. For example, a person filling an interim position may need time to prove their value to an organization.

WHAT STOPS US – Lack of time and resources. The sooner a job is filled, the quicker we can be paid the final fee installment and move on to the next assignment.

BRAND IMAGE – Searchwide is like Prudential — solid as a rock! People like our Midwestern approach, our dependability and quality standards.

SOMETHING THE COMPETITION DOES BETTER – I believe there are times the competition does a better job at listening and understanding needs at the front end of the engagement. I attribute that to our experience in the hospitality industry and being able to anticipate what a client needs. We also need to improve our final presentation of candidates. We do an acceptable job, but we can spend more time at it and truly polish up the final presentation of our candidates.

CUSTOMER SERVICE TOUCH POINT ANALYSIS: Provided by Lisa Galanti, Fitzgerald + CO, www.fitzco.com

DEFINING MOMENT – It happened with our client GA Power Southern Company. We were understaffed as an agency for the first six weeks of taking over this account. Couldn't find the right person on the outside to become the account manager. The client had warned us that they were going to be busy right out of the shoot. For us, first impressions are lasting impressions and we were not giving a great first impression without a dedicated account manager.

LESSON LEARNED – The client's honesty in the beginning turned out for us to be the fastest way to identify a problem. We reorganized internally and took a current account manager off an existing, more mature account and placed them into a new role with GA Power.

DO BUSINESS DIFFERENTLY – Always attempt to introduce the new account manager from the very beginning. This speaks to the importance of maintaining solid people on the bench to step into the game as needs do arise quickly.

MEASURE CUSTOMER SERVICE – We use fresh eyes or a third party to gather the data for us. Clients will talk very openly and candidly with a person not employed by us. This person talks to all the key stakeholders at an account and compiles a book of client impressions and verbatim comments. It is key for us to know if we are meeting the client's expectations. We invest $50,000 a year in this measurement process, but it is a vital investment for our company. The feedback helps us greatly in the area of client retention because it focuses us on building their business. Our mission statement and clear operating values also help in this area as well.

RESULTS SHARED – This book of information is then presented and shared with all the internal company resources to hear the results.

IMPROVE ONE THING – The hiring process and trying to determine up front if the person we want to hire will thrive in the world of advertising. We have to remind ourselves it is important to not get swept away or overly impressed with first and even second impressions/interviews.

BRAND IMAGE – Fitzgerald + CO is a 4-door Mercedes sedan. High quality, strong performance, energetic in the eyes of the customer. We take pride in our craftsmanship. We are not the least expensive, but then again not the most expensive either. We deliver performance!

ONE THING COMPETITION DOES BETTER – Frankly nothing. No one listens better or encourages more healthy dialogue with their clients than Fitzgerald + CO. It is the business philosophy and attitude that literally fuels our growth.

CUSTOMER SERVICE TOUCH POINT ANALYSIS: Provided by Steve Lampa, Senior Vice President Quality Assurance, Marriott Int'l (MI), www.marriott.com

DEFINING MOMENT – The primary performance goals that Marriott measures focus on customer satisfaction. Each Marriott brand has it's own quality assurance process that is driven by customer satisfaction. While MI utilizes a balanced scorecard approach to assess performance in the lodging unit it manages, Customer Satisfaction is the one performance measure that is used to assess performance of all units, whether they are managed by Marriott or by franchisees.

LESSON LEARNED – Customers seem to get it right every time. They know when they are dissatisfied. When a property has poor customer service scores, the systems within are inoperable. If the basic operating systems are not in place, you have problems. If the chain of command doesn't hold people accountable at all levels for customer service, scores do not change. By "systems" we mean operating processes, both those that directly impact customers like cleaning and Maintaining the Hotel, and those that support operations like Training and Development.

DO BUSINESS DIFFERENTLY – Marriott managers know it is not good for their career to have poor customer service scores. Each property has goals and there is an initial test held to measure the system. Once proven statistically valid, all properties have to buy into the process. Initially, there was some resistance to using Guest Service Satisfaction (GSS) scores to determine performance under the QA system. The statistical significance of the scores was questioned early on. However, as management companies began investigating hotels with low customer scores, they saw that customers do get it right. There is now little to no resistance for using this approach for identifying hotels that need improvement.

MEASURE CUSTOMER SERVICE – Marriott Hotels mails out random surveys and receives back more than 100,000 responses per year. Each hotel averages 800 to 1,000 responses per year. The key operations areas to measure include 1) reservation in order, 2) arrival experience, 3) clean room, 4) room maintenance, 5) food and beverage delivery, 6) event delivery, 7) problems experienced and resolved. Since 1995, Marriott has seen steady increases in customer satisfaction company wide. Each Marriott brand has a GSS system similar to the one described above. We are not really unique in our industry. Most of our significant competitors utilize a similar system.

RESULTS SHARED – Most brands release information monthly.

IMPROVE ONE THING – If we could focus on the single point of "reduction of problems experienced," hotels could improve their scores dramatically. We know 23% of guests experience problems and when a customer does report that they experienced a problem, they typically report that they had 2 or 3 of them.

WHAT STOPS YOU FROM DOING IT – The primary impediment is that reducing problems takes a coordinated approach. First, the leadership of the organization must be committed to identifying and eliminating problems. Second, they have to understand how the work of the organization gets done by having clearly defined process maps for key processes. Then you are in a position carry out improvement efforts by collecting information on the kinds of problems you are having and analyzing the data to identify root causes. Root causes should be linked to changes that are needed in the key processes. If you try to solve these problems without changing the underlying processes, the solutions can either be short-lived or can cause other unintended problems.

BRAND IMAGE – Marriott instills confidence in their guests. Marriott's customer service is consistent, offering "no surprise service" by friendly people. We make promises to customers and keep them.

Is there a strong full service competitor out there? Embassy

Suites is smart because travelers do like suites. The concept is straightforward because from the time you check in, you can see and hear where you have to go. Breakfast is the place to just linger, as is the lounge for happy hour. At Embassy Suites, they perform well against basic customer needs, which are a good night's sleep, breakfast, and a place to be with other people.

That, coupled with their 100% satisfaction guarantee, makes them a formidable competitor.

CUSTOMER SERVICE TOUCH POINT ANALYSIS: Provided by Ted Scholz, former Director of Human Resources, San Antonio Marriott Rivercenter & Riverwalk Hotels. Ted Scholz served as the area director of Human Resources for the Marriott Lodging products of San Antonio. He had responsibility for more than 1200 Marriott associates throughout San Antonio.

www.marriott.com

DEFINING MOMENT – A Marriott restaurant wanted to make sure their hostess/greeter would obtain the name of a guest and pass it on to their meal server. The greeter would write down the guest's name on a piece of paper and leave it on the table for the server to pick up.

LESSON LEARNED – Providing good customer service is a talent. Empathy, discernment, caring and being outgoing are examples of talent. Talents are natural in that they are repeated patterns of behavior that you have – like them or not. So the lesson learned is that you hire for talent and train for skill. Though the greeter has the talent for caring because she did want the servers to use the guest's name, Marriott did not teach her the skill of how to actually do it. She thought she was doing the right thing in writing down the guest name for the server, but we realized this is not good service. We learned it was obtrusive for the guest and usually executed poorly on our part. Gimmicks do not work.

DO BUSINESS DIFFERENTLY – We are much more specific in teaching what good service is from a customer standpoint and how to provide the service. For example, we now teach greeters to introduce themselves to a guest and then introduce the guest to the server. Now this is perceived as good service! We also have introduced behavioral interviewing when hiring. We ask potential associates to describe how they would or have behaved in the past. Examples would be: Tell me about a time when you, a customer, or family member, or a friend needed help. How did you help them? Their answer should reveal if they personally helped them or did they refer the problem or avoid it all together. Then you ask for another example . . . do they do it often, did they help someone recently? Behavioral interviewing questions force people to tell you a story when answering a question and allows you to get to the heart of a person's talents.

MEASURE CUSTOMER SERVICE – Mail out Guest Satisfaction Survey to random sampling of guests.

RESULTS SHARED – Scores are tabulated and shared at all department staff meetings, associate meetings, and shift change meetings.

IMPROVE ONE THING – All management needs to walk and talk good customer service. Our financial results will not dictate what the customer expects the service level to be in a Marriott Hotel. In most cases, the execution of good service does not cost much. It is the little things like a smile, a warm heart, and a willingness to serve the public. We have to be careful of the impact a company's profit and loss statement has on customer service. We must remember that the customer's expectations of good customer service do not change.

BRAND IMAGE – Empowered associates with all the resources to anticipate and take care of our customers' unique needs.

COMPETITION DOES BETTER THAN YOU – More individuality in the way service is provided to the customer. For example, many Marriott restaurants have little local flair and do not focus enough on a meal experience.

CUSTOMER SERVICE TOUCH POINT ANALYSIS:
Provided by Jana Love, President ProSolutions Services,
www.prosolutions.net

DEFINING MOMENT – ProSolutions worked very hard obtaining a new customer; over the course of a year we sold them on a shopping service and a training program. The feedback we received on an ongoing basis was extremely positive, then out of the blue the customer said, "We need to scale back and cut $300,000 from our budget and we are going to have to let you go."

LESSON LEARNED – We were forced to re-evaluate the way we were doing business. For example we invested in a full-time manager for this account and ended up giving away thousands of dollars worth of consulting that other companies would have charged for. We also learned that we had so much more to offer and needed to be a company focused on the "Total Customer Experience".

DO BUSINESS DIFFERENTLY – ProSolutions is working to redesign the marketing of the services we offer and charging for services that we have given away in the past. We are the experts in the hospitality industry and we never thought about charging a consulting fee for our expertise. This is a change in our business practice.

MEASURE CUSTOMER SERVICE – Being in the evaluation business, an error-free product is a measurement tool we use with our shoppers, as well as to our customers. Our Account Managers are measured by their responsiveness to more than meet our customers' needs immediately and completely.

RESULTS SHARED – These results are shared through telephone/computer to our shopper. We keep an ongoing record of a yearly error ratio per customer so that this information can be shared. We have accumulated wonderful testimonial letters/quotes abour our customer service.

IMPROVE ONE THING – Staying in front of the technology curve to better serve our customers needs. The challenge in this area remains centered around a variety of requests and capabilities.

WHAT STOPS YOU FROM DOING IT – Capital and workable resources however, we continue to educate ourselves on technology. We have found over the course of 5 years that the options of technology can be a bit like a cosmetic counter.

BRAND IMAGE – ProSolutions is like a chameleon – always changing to meet our customers' needs

SOMETHING YOUR COMPETITION DOES BETTER – Some of our competitors have beaten us in the technology race.

CUSTOMER SERVICE TOUCH POINT ANALYSIS: Provided by David Mackay, President of USPCA – Rio Rancho NM. Customers in this case are defined as members of the United States Personal Chef Association, www.uspca.com.

DEFINING MOMENT – In the mid-90's, USPCA hired John Moore onto the staff. John's background in printing and graphics helped the association make a huge breakthrough in adding value through member services. USPCA decided to expand from a four-page newsletter to a 10-page magazine. Today, the magazine has been expanded to more than forty pages. Many members comment it is the most valuable part of being a USPCA member and they read it cover-to-cover the same day it arrives!

LESSON LEARNED – The more information that we communicate in a high quality format, whether it is through training materials or the magazine, the more highly the members value the association.

DO BUSINESS DIFFERENTLY – We take a high quality approach to everything we do. We know that the happier our members are, the more they renew and the more they are willing to pay for services, conferences, training, etc. We have also improved the quality of our web site in terms of how we disseminate information.

MEASURE MEMBER SERVICE – We track every member call that comes in with a service question. Just a few years ago, our staff was spending upwards of half of their time each day on the phone answering members' questions. Today with the improvement of everything from our magazine, web site and local chapter meetings, we have greatly reduced the number of member inquires via telephone. Our renewal rate is approximately 40% after two full years of membership. We constantly strive to improve upon this important figure.

IMPROVE ONE THING – Personal liability insurance can be expensive for personal chefs. We are announcing a new program that will include up to $1 million in personal liability insurance as part of a membership fee.

WHAT STOPS US – The only thing that will stop this insurance benefit from rolling out is if we don't prove to the chefs the value of the liability policy. We need everyone to see the amount of money they can save by all participating in our insurance program.

BRAND IMAGE – "We earn our reputation one chef at a time."

SOMETHING THE COMPETITION DOES BETTER – There are six other personal chefs associations out there. We are far and away the largest. This means smaller associations can be more personalized to their membership. As an example, some hold weekly chat groups where they exchange recipes, etc. We are simply too large to do that. We depend upon our local chapters and the member exchange board on our web site to stay connected – along with our fabulous magazine!

CUSTOMER SERVICE TOUCH POINT ANALYSIS:
Provided by Tom Cowperthwaite, formerly, Director of MIS
Applications, Cox Communications, www.cox.com.

This touch point is from an "internal customer service" perspective. During a three-year period, Cox experienced tremendous growth and essentially doubled in size. In conjunction with that, technology assumed a greater role in the strategic direction of the company. As a result, technology and business became very intertwined and internal customers began to come to MIS looking for strategic solutions for their business issues.

DEFINING MOMENT – The demand for IT support increased dramatically as new products were introduced and more business processes were automated. MIS personnel became inundated with requests from virtually every department in the organization. Cox did not have a formal project management process in place. This caused a great deal of confusion regarding projects and their lifecycle. The defining moment occurred when MIS developed our own Application Development Methodology to provide a standardized framework for all systems development at Cox. It defined the activities associated with each phase of a project and the roles of the team members. What this forced our internal customers to do was decide in advance 1) what the high-level business requirements are for the project; 2) how the project fits into the overall strategic direction of the company; 3) if the project business case is cost justified and 4) the priorities for what had to be done first, second, third, etc., within the project.

LESSON LEARNED – Instead of MIS trying to do everything, it forced our internal customers to take a more active role in the development process. As the sponsor, they were assigned additional responsibilities and assumed joint-ownership for the success of the project.

DO BUSINESS DIFFERENTLY – Customers no longer came to MIS with a long wish list. Instead they had to define their requirements in advance and prioritize their development requests. Sponsors were required to submit a product description and business case for each of their initiatives. As a result, fewer projects were requested and approved and approved projects were initiated quicker.

MEASURE INTERNAL CUSTOMER SERVICE – Quarterly I would meet with the VP of "Customer Cares" to discuss project expectations, timelines and results. She would explain issues such as call routing and length of calls in the field call centers. At other times we tackled Cox phone systems projects focused on pay-per-view movie systems and on-line billing. I would listen and explain the resources available and possibly the limitations we faced in MIS. These formalized quarterly meetings went a long way in enhancing lines of communication and meeting internal customer expectations.

Annually, employee satisfaction surveys are completed and 25% of my incentive pay was based on internal customer satisfaction results.

RESULTS SHARED – The quarterly meeting results were shared with my direct reports. Between quarterly meetings, any urgent issues were communicated immediately. Upon completion of any project, customer service surveys were sent out by MIS to measure satisfaction. Results would come back anonymously and were shared with all appropriate employees.

IMPROVE ONE THING – Better alignment of MIS projects with the strategic direction and priorities of the company. Often times the field priorities were different than those of corporate. Likewise, the priorities of one department at corporate were different than those of another department.

BRAND IMAGE – MIS at Cox Communications is like a Timex watch – we take a licking and keep on ticking! We were responsive and dedicated, but we didn't always say yes to every project. We believed strongly in enhancing business processes, but not every process could be automated!

ONE THING COMPETITION DOES BETTER – Most cable companies already have the formalized cost benefit analysis and Application Development Methodology in place. What Cox needs to do is change their internal structure to better serve their growing corporate needs as well as their 6.2 million external customers.

CUSTOMER SERVICE TOUCH POINT ANALYSIS:
Provided by Charlie Tompkey, Real Estate Agent, REMAX
Xecutex, Oakton VA, www.xecutex.com

DEFINING MOMENT – In an attempt to balance my business and create name recognition, I elected to advertise my real estate services at George Mason University in Fairfax VA. Specifically I chose the University athletic program and their men and women's basketball. This source now accounts for nearly 43% of my business and a great increase in clients.

LESSON LEARNED – I realized that without support staff to provide great client service, there could be a decrease in my business over time. So, I formed THE TOMPKEY TEAM with an administrative coordinator and partner.

DO BUSINESS DIFFERENTLY – I am now organized so that my clients know that I have the time to meet all their needs – in a timely fashion.

MEASURE CUSTOMER SERVICE – In real estate, it is rather simple – it is all based on referrals. The most important way to measure service is to track the number of referrals you receive from satisfied clients. I think of my client list as a forest. We track every referral to its origin. A "solid client" is a root client. A tree is simply a "client." A person who is referred is thought of as a branch. The word picture is that a root client refers often and a tree client often comes from a root client. Branches come from both roots and trees. The size of the forest depends on the amount of planting and nourishing we do of our roots and trees.

IMPROVE ONE THING – I need to put myself in front of more people and create additional opportunities to sell our services and myself.

Brand image – The Beatles sang it best "I get by with a little help from my friends." Once you are a client, we help with anything you need and that is what friends do!

SOMETHING THE COMPETITION DOES BETTER – The essence of a real estate agent is to represent a client's best interests in all aspects of the transaction whether buying, selling, renting or investing. No client has told me that anyone does this with more passion or care than TEAM TOMPKEY.

Charlie Tompkey is extremely proud of a transaction that resulted in a very happy client. A "root client" from UU Net referred a new "tree client" (Gail and Dean) that had not been working with an agent before contacting Charlie. They had been looking for what agents call a "character home." The couple wanted lots of land in a very private area – close to public access! They thought they had found their "dream house" the day before they called Charlie and simply wanted him to assist in the purchase process. Working together, they wrote a contract but eventually lost the house when they were outbid by $15,000.

So, Charlie went to work and previewed more than 15 homes in the Haymarket VA area. He found what he hoped would be another "dream house" and Gail agreed but Dean was concerned about the commute and they lost out when the house sold very quickly. Now it was becoming very emotional and Gail had literally given up on her dream.

Soon thereafter, a house popped up on Charlie's computer within one hour of being listed. Gail and Charlie saw it within 48 hours and both agreed it was perfect. The problem was Dean was away (playing golf) and couldn't be reached effectively on his cell phone. So Charlie and Gail wrote a contract anyway with an escalating clause to solidify the transaction. The contract went through two days later, subject to home inspection, without Dean ever seeing the house! I told you at the start that this has a happy ending! In the end both Gail AND Dean love the house and that makes Charlie extremely happy and proud.

CUSTOMER SERVICE TOUCH POINT ANALYSIS:

Provided by Michael Gehrisch, President & CEO, International
Association of Convention & Visitor Bureaus (IACVB)
Washington, D.C. IACVB is a trade association representing
more than 800 convention and visitors bureaus around the
globe. www.iacvb.com

DEFINING MOMENT – I believe you can learn customer
service lessons by observing other organizations that truly "get
it" and Southwest Airlines is a case in point. Four days after
the September 11 tragedy, I was probably number 250 in line
in Baltimore to board a Southwest flight. In my mind, I was
thinking there is time to make this flight, but I'm thirsty and at
some point will likely need to use a restroom. All of a sudden,
a couple of Southwest employees wheeled by a cart that had
been converted to carry drinks and snacks. This brought a
smile to all our faces. What made it better was when the
employees announced that they would also act as "designated
stand-ins" for people while they went to the bathroom! This is
not "policy" for the airline, but rather two Southwest
employees providing personalized customer service – the best
way they knew how – and using the limited resources
available to them.

LESSON LEARNED – In the trade association business we
should expect our staff to provide personalized or customized
service whenever dealing with a member. Do what it takes to
make them happy!

DO BUSINESS DIFFERENTLY – We are fundamentally
rethinking our business approach. What that means, in a
practical sense, is that we reintroduce the pieces that work
extremely well to our members and rebuild those pieces that
do not work well.

MEASURE CUSTOMER SERVICE – Members respond via
e-mail and phone to technology-based events and use written
surveys to critique conferences.

RESULTS SHARED – They are shared as soon as possible with staff, speakers, and attendees. The objective is to share the information quickly enough so we may react before our next event to demonstrate that we listened and care about feedback.

IMPROVE ONE THING – Provide members with more information as to how IACVB can help them build and manage their bureau.

WHAT STOPS US – A lack of customized feedback information and staff resources to gather and respond on a timely basis.

BRAND IMAGE – IACVB delivers consistent value! To our members we must appear innovative, contemporary, fresh, and friendly. We need to understand what makes us different from other associations that people belong to and exploit our unique value proposition.

SOMETHING THE COMPETITION DOES BETTER – There are competing trade associations that do a better job reflecting a return on a member's investment. We need to be able to communicate the ROI and be a part of the financial investment decision.

OTHER BOOKS AVAILABLE FROM
APPLIED BUSINESS COMMUNICATIONS:

LICENSE TO SELL
Professional Field Guide to
Selling Skills & Market Trends
ISBN 0-9654362-2-5

by
Joe Ilvento & Doug Price
$29.95

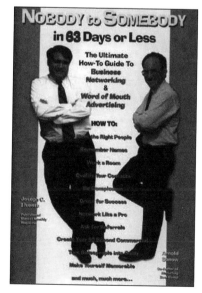

NOBODY TO SOMEBODY IN
63 DAYS OR LESS
The Ultimate How-To Guide
to Business Networking &
Word of Mouth Advertising
ISBN 0-9654362-0-9

by
Joseph C. Ilvento
Arnold Sanow
$29.95

To order, contact either author for book purchases and volume discounts. Books are also available on amazon.com or by contacting your local bookstore.

License to Sell
Professional Field Guide to Selling Skills & Market Trends

Joe Ilvento and Doug Price have joined forces to bring you the latest selling trends that are revolutionizing the way we do business. The Internet and e-commerce have replaced traditional selling channels, and this book will give you the insight and strategy you need to succeed. The electronic world we live in today is moving at warp speed and those who are able to recognize sales opportunities will be able to ride this electronic tidal wave for years to come. But along with *strategy* you need *skills*. *License to Sell* will provide you with valuable, need-to-know sales ideas and concepts. You'll master skills on how to:

Prospect

Probe

Qualify

Present

Close

Follow-up

Negotiate

And More...

This book is a must-read for anyone whose goal is to become a true sales professional operating in both traditional and electronic selling environments.

The proven strategies and techniques are easy to implement and will put money in your pocket for years to come. To remain successful, salespeople must incorporate modern-day tools such as the Internet, cell phones, personal digital assistants, and hand-held computers into their overall selling strategies. This book provides a glimpse into the future of selling and reveals secrets you can use to outsmart your competition now and in the future.

License to Sell is really two books in one. The first book focuses on *18 Sales Trends* that will dramatically impact the way you do business now and into the future. The second book covers *over 20 core selling techniques and concepts* that, when applied, will allow you to outsell your competition every time.

This essential resource provides:

Easy to Read and Apply Concepts

Interactive Exercises

Top Secret Sales Tips

e-Commerce Trends

Suggested Phrases

Proven Sales Formulas

Negotiation Strategies

Closing Techniques

The Secrets to Sales Success

License to Sell and *License to Serve* will prepare any kind of organization — from public to private and profit to non-profit — with the necessary skills to exceed customer needs and expectations to increase profitability.

Table of Contents at a glance:

Sales Trends

Sales Skills

BEFORE THE SALE

Prospecting 101 and Beyond
Prospecting for New Customers
The Art of Asking Questions
Qualifying — It's All in the Questions
Outbound Telemarketing is Proactive
Gatekeepers & Voice Mail
The Sales Cycle

DURING THE SALE

Relationship Building: You are the Initial Product
Customer Traits
Benefit Selling: Transitioning from Features to Tactical Benefits
Adding Value to What You Sell
Selling Against the Competition
Buying Signals
Psychology & Traits of the Super Salesperson
The Art of Closing

AFTER THE SALE

How to Turn Objections into Opportunities
Negotiation Skills
Put Yourself Next in Line
Follow-Up — You'll Be Hearing from Me

NOBODY TO SOMEBODY IN 63 DAYS OR LESS
The Ultimate How-To Guide to Business Networking & Word of Mouth Advertising

Joseph C. Ilvento and Arnold Sanow have teamed up to bring you over 100 personal and professional networking strategies, tips and techniques. If you consider yourself now to be an avid networker, this book will double your effectiveness practically overnight. If you are new to the networking scene or want to tap into the free world of word of mouth advertising, you couldn't ask for a better book to read.

In 186 pages, you'll learn how to:

Boost your career to new heights in less time

Turn everyone you know into a salesperson for you

Create a positive reputation that precedes you

Learn how to double and triple your return on leads

Demystify the networking process

Build a contact database your competitors will envy

Never pay for traditional advertising again

It's not a question of which strategy you will use, but how many. Within 63 days, you'll find yourself using 10, 15, 30 or more of these strategies to maximize your personal effectiveness with everyone you meet.

Making it big in business today is easy if you know the right people. The sooner you meet them, the sooner you achieve success. For most, it takes a lifetime. For those of you who read this book, 63 days or less.

Knowing what to say and how to say it is a skill. Make a good impression on someone and where you go from there is up to you.

Each page is full of how-to advice on ways to grow your business and increase profits. The book covers everything from handshakes to thank you notes. This is definitely one of those books you hope your competition never reads.

Make Yourself Memorable: 17 Strategies

Harness the Power of Listening: 11 Check Points

Develop a 60-Second Commercial

Ask 10 Power Questions to Uncover Needs

Choose the Right People to Sit Next to

Become a Networking Magnet

Earn as Much in One Morning as You Do in One Day

It's who you know that counts! Learn the secrets the pros have been using for years to put money in their pockets. Learn what just a few hours a week combined with some expert networking strategies can do to boost your contacts. You have nothing to lose and only friendships to gain.

"A must read, *License to Sell*, provided the roadmap for me to create a very lucrative Real Estate career, a business that was new to me just a few years ago. As a real estate professional in a very competitive and diverse market, I must differentiate myself. Most do it through discounted fees; I do it through exceptional customer service. *License to Serve* will help everyone to close the loop on successful transactions and secure future business and referrals."

— **Bob Gojkovich Jr.**, Russ Lyon Realty Company

"Whether you are managing your internal customers or serving external customers, *License to Serve* holds the wisdom and directives on how to make it happen."

— **Lisa Marie Main**, Executive Coach and Organizational Consultant
Continuum Consulting Services, LLC

"Even as a small business owner, this book has helped my company in very big ways!"

— **Thomas Piasio**, Owner
Copy Quick Inc.

"If you can't find at least ten messages in this book to help you nurture your relationships with your customers, then you better check your pulse."

— **Phil Genovese**, Manager of Customer Care
for the world's largest transportation company

"Although we refer to them as constituents rather than customers, the need to serve remains the same. An independent educational institution cannot remain vibrant without, communication with and participation from, parents and alumni. *License to Serve* provides the action steps needed to proactively address the needs of our key constituent groups."

— **Timothy R. Cottrell, Ph.D.**, Chief Communications & Information Officer, The Lawrenceville School